DESIGNING A WORLD FOR EVERYONE

30 Years of Inclusive Design

With best wishes
Jeremy Myerson

LUND HUMPHRIES

Jeremy Myerson

First published in 2021 by Lund Humphries

Lund Humphries
Office 3, Book House
261A City Road
London EC1V 1JX
UK

www.lundhumphries.com

Designing a World for Everyone: 30 Years of Inclusive Design © Jeremy Myerson, 2021
All rights reserved

ISBN: 978–1–84822–463–6

A Cataloguing-in-Publication record for this book is available from the British Library.

All rights reserved. No part of this publication may be reproduced, stored in a retrieval system or transmitted in any form or by any means, electrical, mechanical or otherwise, without first seeking the permission of the copyright owners and publishers. Every effort has been made to seek permission to reproduce the images in this book. Any omissions are entirely unintentional, and details should be addressed to the publishers.

Jeremy Myerson has asserted his right under the Copyright, Designs and Patent Act, 1988, to be identified as the Author of this Work.

Front cover: Foyle Reeds installation on bridge over the River Foyle, Northern Ireland. Visualisation by Ralf Alwani and Greg Edwards, Urban Scale Interventions. See River, page 94.

Copy edited by Pamela Bertram
Designed by Jacqui Cornish
Cover design by Stefi Orazi
Proofread by Patrick Cole
Set in Circular Std
Printed in Slovenia

Contents

Foreword by Helen Hamlyn 4
Foreword by Jony Ive 5

Introduction 6

Airport 12
Ambulance 16
Bank 22
Bathroom 26
Beer Glass 32
Bus Stop 34
Care Home 36
Classroom 42
Crutch 44
Desk 46
Food Pack 49
Garden 51
Garment 53
Hospital 58
Kitchen 68

Light 70
Medication 74
Mobile Phone 77
Office 81
Park 87
Power Tool 89
Public Toilet 91
River 94
Scooter 102
Stairlift 106
Street 109
Taxi 114
Typeface 118
Vehicle 120
Wheelchair 128

Project Credits 132
Acknowledgements 141
Index 142
Illustration Credits 144

Foreword

In the 1950s, history tells me that I was the Royal College of Art's youngest student. Today, I am probably one of the College's oldest supporters and benefactors. My relationship with the RCA has been a rich, multi-faceted and enduring one: it goes back to training as a designer in the Fashion and Textiles department and moves on to the momentous decision I developed some decades later to initiate a new programme dedicated to improving everyday design for older people, improving their quality of life and helping them to live independently for longer.

Thirty years ago, in 1991, the RCA agreed with me to set up the DesignAge programme at the College, supported by my charitable trust. My own experiences made me very much aware of the sense of social responsibility that designers needed to develop at this formative stage in their career. DesignAge was the logical continuation of a process that started with an exhibition in 1986 at the V&A's Boilerhouse Gallery in London, *New Design for Old*, co-curated by myself and architect Elisabeth Henderson, which showed how design could make a difference to the lives of older people, allowing them to live longer at home which most wished to do. Sixteen of the world's leading industrial designers at that time generously contributed designs for this exhibition.

DesignAge became the first step towards the Helen Hamlyn Centre for Design. The new centre was launched to develop ideas for people who can be overlooked by designers due to age or disability. My concern was that our new design research venture at the RCA should address the needs of these marginalised groups by developing practical applications of academic and creative thinking in co-operation with commercial partners and made easily available.

This book explores how this mission took shape. I am very impressed to see how the principles of inclusive design have developed over this 30-year period. Looking at some of the centre's most important projects, which are discussed in this volume, from the redesign of the emergency ambulance to significant interventions in the kitchen, bathroom, workplace and streetscape, the Helen Hamlyn Centre for Design has combined social activism with creative thinking and business application in a distinctive and influential way. It is now influential globally.

The author, Jeremy Myerson, has been at the heart of our work throughout this 30-year history. But as Jeremy is the first to acknowledge in these pages, this has been a tremendous team effort. So, I want to thank all the talented students, graduates, researchers, faculty members and partners at the RCA who have contributed to a body of work that I hope will inspire other people and institutions around the world to design a better world for everyone. For all that has been achieved, there is still so much more to do.

Lady Hamlyn
Founder and Chair
Helen Hamlyn Trust

Foreword

The Royal College of Art is renowned for its ability to imagine a world not yet in existence and for the extraordinary breadth and diversity of the work it produces. Design at the RCA comes in many brilliant colours and different forms – and one of the most distinctive and enduring of these is the Helen Hamlyn Centre for Design, the College's longest-running unit for design research.

Over a 30-year period, starting in 1991, the centre has pioneered the practice of inclusive design, exploring what it means to make every aspect of our world more accessible to people of all ages and abilities. Through left-field creative enquiry, sustained innovation and participatory methods, it has transformed an area of design that once stood outside the mainstream and was given a wide berth by many designers.

This book, written by the centre's co-founder and former Director Jeremy Myerson, uses 30 everyday objects and environments as a way to demonstrate the impact the Helen Hamlyn Centre for Design's research has had on the world around us. Many of the projects, especially related to medical technology, show how moments of creativity can be sparked through multi-disciplinary collaboration between designers and engineers, clinicians and social scientists. If we want to live in a world that works for all of us, the future will be all about this type of imaginative, creative interaction – generating processes and viewpoints which are surprisingly connective, and shockingly new.

It is a privilege to spend time with these projects, and as somebody who is eternally optimistic about the future of making and the importance of design in technological development, turning the pages of this book is a humbling, reassuring and inspiring experience.

Recording 30 years of the Helen Hamlyn Centre for Design is not just an achievement for the Royal College of Art but a milestone for Helen Hamlyn, who initiated the centre with the RCA and whose Trust was the founder funder and has continued to support the centre at every stage of its development throughout its history. We're all hugely grateful to the Trust and to Helen personally, herself an RCA alumna, for having the vision and the tenacity to show how the power of design can make a difference to our lives.

Sir Jony Ive KBE
Chancellor
Royal College of Art

Introduction

During a project to design a system to guide people through the cavernous spaces of the soon-to-be-built Terminal 5 at Heathrow Airport, I once entertained a meeting of senior managers from British Airports Authority with the results of our ethnographic research. Our most important observation, I explained, was that older people go to the toilet a lot in airport terminals. Tell us something we don't know, they laughed. Well, I said, do you want to know why they go so often? They go to the loo to hear flight announcements. They have trouble listening to announcements and reading information in large, busy, open concourses – ceramic-clad toilets have perfect sound and close-up graphics, so they can concentrate.

That insight led to a proposal from the design team I was leading to create 'acoustic arches' in Terminal 5 – small, independent pieces of micro-architecture within the concourse, lined with ceramic tiles. These information booths, or caves, are today commonplace in many of Europe's airport terminals, branded by advertisers and popular with passengers of all ages. It just goes to show that study of seniors with poor eyesight and hearing, who sit outside the mainstream travelling public, can, surprisingly, serve as an alternative route to mainstream innovation.

I tell this story – one of many you will find in this book – because it is easy to forget that the way we experience the world is largely through the design of the places, products, communications, services and systems we encounter every day. Design determines how difficult or easy it is to achieve certain things: whether boarding a plane, taking a bath, cooking a meal, crossing the street or making a call on a smartphone, we all want a world that works for us all the time. However, some people are excluded from the simplest and most basic everyday experiences. Why? This is because the act of designing has given insufficient consideration to their level of physical ability or cognitive difference or cultural background or economic circumstance.

There are deep-rooted reasons why this should be so. The story of design over the past 100 years is entwined in the development of mass production, mass markets and mass media – an economic growth system unprecedented in human history. To make this system work, designers were required to treat people as target customers and segment them into broad and conveniently framed social-economic groups for the purposes of marketing. This is not to say that there was no user research – there was plenty. But it concentrated on the consumer mainstream; those on the margins or extremes of need, such as older and disabled people, for example, were not even included in the frame of reference.

What made design so important to the era of mass everything was its two essential contributions to business: visual abstraction, which enabled sellers to offer a simple brand proposition that would be instantly recognisable across different regions, languages and cultures; and scaling up, which created economies of production so that a single solution could service billions of customers. From mass market shavers to mass market cars, corporate logos, retail store rollouts and global office space plans, we have seen this process played out in every city on the planet.

Over the past 30 years, however, there has been a backlash against a uniform mass market approach in which one size fits all. Today, it is increasingly accepted that such a basis for designing can exclude large numbers of people who don't conform to the norm. Abstraction blinds designers to the realities and contradictions of people's lives. Scaling up limits the scope for customisable design to meet real needs and desires. The focus in design has therefore switched from learning just a little about very large groups of people in order to design for mass markets, to learning a great deal about relatively small numbers of people, concentrating not on what makes them similar, but on what makes them different.

Within this context, designers have stopped the pretence of maintaining a scientific neutrality in their work and started to engage at the most empathic and human level with the people who will experience and use their designs. They have brought a new mindset to designing, one that is participatory as opposed to expert. Individuals and communities have ceased to be lab rats studied from behind a two-way mirror, but partners in an open co-design process, their expertise in relation to their own lived experience every bit as valuable as the skills that the professional designer brings to any project.

This new movement in design has a broad descriptor: inclusive design. It is an approach aimed at designing the things around us for maximum benefit by the maximum number of people, including those on the margins and not in the mainstream. Its emphasis is on delving deeply into specific human experiences to address needs and aspirations, as opposed to fixing quickly on general preferences and assumptions to find a market. And its philosophy is that the individual is not excluded from his or her environment due to any inherent deficiencies they might have – they are disabled only by the thoughtlessness of its design. Empathy with human experience is the hard currency of inclusive design.

As a term, inclusive design was first discussed in an academic paper given at an ergonomics conference in Toronto in 1994. The author was Roger Coleman, the designer and social activist with whom I co-founded the Helen Hamlyn Centre for Design at the Royal College of Art. In defining inclusive design in the early 1990s as a philosophy and a practice, Coleman gave the Helen Hamlyn Centre for Design its driving force. Working within the unique creative community of the Royal College of Art, the centre would go on to build an extensive portfolio of collaborative projects over a long period, pioneering new methods, coaching designers at all levels in the approach and bringing a more inclusive way of thinking about design to international attention.

This book therefore maps a movement and marks a milestone at the same time. The movement is the rise of inclusive design over a 30-year period from 1991 to 2021. The milestone is the 30th anniversary of the Helen Hamlyn Centre for Design in 2021. I have chosen to show the parameters of inclusive design through the lens of the centre's own projects in the field. To do this, I've picked 30 everyday artefacts and places and explored our influence on them. These cases vary in scale. Some are simple, hand-held objects such as a shatterproof beer glass, a jam jar with a square lid for easy opening or a carbon-fibre crutch. Others form part of large and complex environments or systems – the care home, hospital, streetscape, riverfront or airport, for example.

Many of the creative ideas discussed in this book have seen the light of day as products on the market or as public services – from the all-in-one care station at the foot of the hospital bed, the lighting system for inner-city housing estates and the open-data website to locate a public toilet, to a typeface for dyslexic children and a garden for autistic adults. Others are demonstrator projects, educating the market in the art of the possible and influencing producers and service providers to incorporate certain features. Safer streets, sensual bathrooms, accessible parks and graphic guidance for drug packaging all fall into this second grouping. A third category we can file under 'ideas for the future' – such as a public swimming pool sited right in the middle of an airport or an electric car which lights the street and redirects lost tourists when parked. All the projects, however, are equally valid in reflecting an approach which could be described as designing *with* people, as opposed to designing *for* people.

* * *

Stories about how research centres are set up inside art schools or universities are usually less significant in the great scheme of things than the knowledge they produce. But it is worth sharing here some background on the origins of the Helen Hamlyn Centre for Design. It all started with the landmark *New Design for Old* exhibition in 1986 in the Boilerhouse Gallery of the Victoria & Albert Museum, the forerunner to the Design Museum.

Curators Helen Hamlyn and Elizabeth Henderson invited 14 international designers to redesign everyday items for the home to suit the needs of older people. Helen Hamlyn was motivated by her struggles at the time to keep her own mother living independently in her home and out of institutional care following an accident. Helen couldn't find the products she wanted on the market, so she used the exhibition as a platform to commission some new ones and give manufacturers a wake-up call. *New Design for Old* was an unexpected success, hugely popular with the public.

As a designer herself and an alumna of the Royal College of Art (RCA) in fashion and textiles, Helen Hamlyn subsequently directed her own charitable foundation to support a new action-based research unit on design for ageing populations at the RCA called DesignAge. This was founded in 1991 under the direction of Roger Coleman and it became both a precursor and a prototype for a new research centre for design at the RCA that would bear her name. So began the first of four distinct phases of the Helen Hamlyn Centre for Design. Between 1991 and 1998, Coleman led a period of agenda-setting and definition. DesignAge won the Queen's Award for Higher Education in 1995, which turned heads, and began a series of industrial collaborations which set a template for combining social activism with commercial application.

I first became involved in the work of DesignAge in the early 1990s when I chaired a product challenge event at the RCA with member design firms from the Design Business Association. The atmosphere was electric. Everyone wanted to get involved. Among the standout concepts on show that night was an inclusive rethink of the urban bus by IDEO, whose proposals were subsequently taken up by Transport for London. In 1998, DesignAge broadened its scope to become a fully fledged research centre dedicated to the then-emerging study and practice of inclusive design. I joined as co-founder and co-director alongside Roger Coleman. So began the Helen Hamlyn Centre for Design's second phase – a period of activation (1999–2007) in which we encouraged the College's brightest young students and graduates to actively engage with the design needs of more diverse groups. In Helen Hamlyn's words: 'Make things people want; don't just make people want things.'

One of our big ideas was to recast design for ageing within the RCA as 'design for our future selves'. The message was that this will happen to all of us. We had already initiated a student award scheme to reward the best work and we were much taken with the words of the gerontologist Bernard Isaacs who said: 'Design for the young and you exclude the old; design for the old and you include everyone.' We resolved that the needs of people who are ageing should set the inclusive standard by which all design should be judged. We also recognised that the imaginative work-arounds that people with disabilities used just to cope with the difficulties of daily life comprised a special form of creativity from which we could learn.

Another big idea became the 'engine' that drove the centre: every year we employed around ten new RCA graduates as Helen Hamlyn Research Associates, teaming them with partners in business and industry to explore new ideas addressing demographic change. At a time when there was general consensus around getting engineers and social scientists to think and act like designers, our modus operandi was to do exactly the opposite. We took highly skilled designers in a range of disciplines (from graphics and textiles to architecture, product design, vehicle design and design engineering) and showed them how to think and act like social scientists – our belief was that they should learn just enough about ethnographic research to capture user requirements and then take those insights into a creative design process.

This phase of the centre saw some familiar targets for innovation and improvement – better kitchens and bathrooms for older people, better furniture and wheelchairs. We had an early market success with a set of low-cost, lightweight power tools for the home commissioned by B&Q, which became bestsellers in the UK and China. But as the digital revolution took shape, so our collaborations began to focus on technological inclusion. We were amazed to discover that digital service providers were making exactly the same mistakes with older customers as kitchen and bathroom manufacturers had done many years before.

Healthcare became another growing area of interest, as older and disabled people are disproportionally reliant on safe, innovative healthcare services, and can be seen as lead or extreme users in this context. Roger Coleman led the charge, co-authoring an influential report in 2003 on how the NHS should take a more strategic approach to design. We subsequently became involved in several landmark NHS projects – to redesign the emergency ambulance, to reduce violence and aggression in A&E, and to reduce medical error on surgical wards.

* * *

Upon Roger Coleman's retirement at the end of 2007, the centre entered its third phase under my sole direction. This was a period of intensification (2008–2015) as we deepened our theoretical grasp of inclusive design with a new PhD programme and several grants from UK research councils, and extended our work into larger-scale collaborative projects. The Helen Hamlyn Trust extended its support for our work with the RCA's first endowed Chair of Design, a post which I have the privilege of holding today. Our partnership with Imperial College London on healthcare projects led directly to a new design-led innovation unit on the healthcare frontline at St Mary's Hospital in London, the Helix Centre.

Under our senior research fellow Julia Cassim, our partnership with the Design Business Association on the DBA Inclusive Design Challenge was extended into a series of 48-hour and 24 hour challenge workshops which were taken all over the world. Workplace design also came to the fore as the pensions crisis forced up the retirement age and extended working lives at a stroke – we developed a programme of research to create a more inclusive, human-centred workplace based around wellbeing and the senses.

After I stood down as director in 2015, the Helen Hamlyn Centre for Design entered its fourth phase under my successor Rama Gheerawo, who joined the centre on the same day as me and served for many years as my deputy. This was a period of augmentation (2015–2021) as Gheerawo, a design engineer by training, boldly led the centre into new territory. Projects were aligned more closely to computer and material science, exploring the use of digital apps, autonomous vehicles, smart textiles and virtual reality. The scope of inclusive design – once narrowly cast around physical disability – was broadened to include issues of mental health, race and social equity. However, the heritage of the centre was not forgotten. In 2020, we received a large research grant from the government to establish the Design Age Institute, a new initiative to create innovations for an ageing society. This is where we find ourselves today, circling back to *New Design for Old* and the birth of DesignAge in 1991. It feels like a good place to be.

In all four phases of the Helen Hamlyn Centre for Design, Helen Hamlyn herself and her Trust have been ever-present. Helen has great instincts as a designer and a visionary sense of what is about to become important – her tenacity and passion to create a better world for everyone has been an inspiration. It is indeed exceptional to provide support over such a sustained period of 30 years in the way that the Helen Hamlyn Trust has done.

I have tried to represent all four phases of the centre in selecting projects for this book. The body of work shown here is drawn from our burgeoning RCA community of research associates, PhD candidates, student award winners, post-doctoral researchers and project leads, as well as from the DBA's roster of design firms. It is the work of a great many talented people from whom I have learnt a lot and to whom I owe a great debt. In the interests of readability, I have used 'we' in the main narrative but all are listed in the credits.

Early in the life of the centre, I was asked if our work would be done when people could just refer to 'design' rather than 'inclusive design' and automatically expect an inclusive approach. We're not there yet, but after 30 years, we can confidently say we're some way down the road.

overleaf

Helen Hamlyn Research Associates in action: Katie Gaudion and Andrew Brand (top left) develop sensory toys for use in autism research; Jamie Tunnard (below left) rethinks video conferencing; Lisa Johansson and Catherine Greene (centre) explore local community networks; Tom Stables (top right) investigates the world of hearing tests; and Maja Kecman and Karina Torlei (bottom right) redesign the neck brace

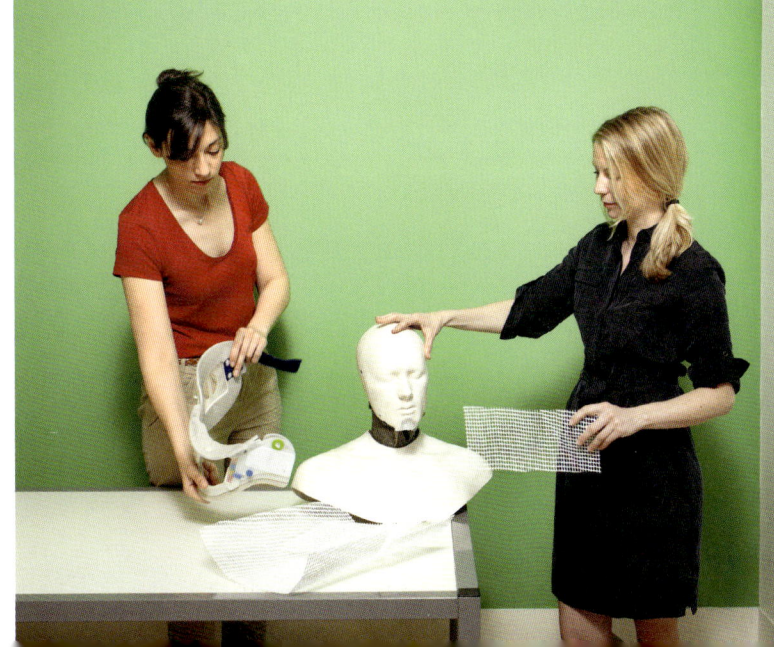

Airport

Imagine Europe's largest new airport terminal is under construction and a team of architectural researchers from the Royal College of Art proposes to the developer that a large public swimming pool should be placed tantalisingly in the middle of it. Is this an outlandish creative idea or a logical, human-centred response to the brief? The airport terminal in question is Terminal 5 at Heathrow, the year is 2000, and the research team based in the Helen Hamlyn Centre for Design is trying to figure out how to make the gigantic split-level superstructure – designed by architects Richard Rogers Partnership – easier to navigate by the travelling public, a growing proportion of whom will be older and disabled people according to demographic predictions.

The writer J.G. Ballard famously said of airports: 'The terminal concourses are the *ramblas* and *agoras* of the future city, time-free zones where all the clocks of the world are displayed; an atlas of arrival and destinations forever updating itself, where briefly we become true world citizens.' But the research team on the project quickly formed a far less favourable and forgiving view of the generic airport concourse – one that is busy but banal, artificial and exhausting, offering little to the traveller by way of interest or delight that might raise the spirits or revive the body while they wait to board a plane. A programme of user research, shadowing people with a range of physical and visual impairments as they tried to carry out various tasks in existing Heathrow terminals, confirmed how difficult, confusing and soul-destroying the whole experience could become.

British Airports Authority (BAA) commissioned the RCA research team, in one of the earliest large-scale collaborations for the new Helen Hamlyn Centre for Design, because it was concerned that navigation of Terminal 5 should be as easy and intuitive as possible for people of all ages and abilities. BAA's design brief talked about creating 'the world's most refreshing interchange'. Its list of aspirations included 'an inspired sense of place', 'pockets of memorable delight', 'calm expectancy' and 'glide through to fly through'. Based on the results of our user-shadowing research and visits to other airports, it became clear that a radical alternative to a purely functional glass-and-steel-box approach to terminal design might be required.

As a provocation, the researchers suggested siting an Olympic-sized swimming pool on the lower level to act as a navigational anchor for the entire terminal. The sounds of water splashing and children laughing, and the wafts of chlorine and bath salts would serve not only as an orientation device within the vast hangar-like space but also create a public amenity for travellers to refresh, recharge and exercise between flights, especially long haul. If this was an extreme proposal at the outer edges of design research for wayfinding – and one that BAA would politely reject for reasons of practicality – it nevertheless opened up a wider debate about what a 'refreshing interchange' really meant.

At our suggestion, BAA pivoted to a new position, which we named 'process to pleasure'. The Terminal 5 airport concourse was reimagined as a 'sensory landscape' comprising a series of autonomous elements that would provide information, orientation and comfort at different points. These elements included tactile pathways, over-sized furniture pieces and retail kiosks, as well as an innovation called the 'audio arch'. The idea behind the audio arch was to create an enclosed piece of micro-architecture on the concourse that would present travel information with super-large graphics and high-fidelity sound within a ceramic-

AIRPORT

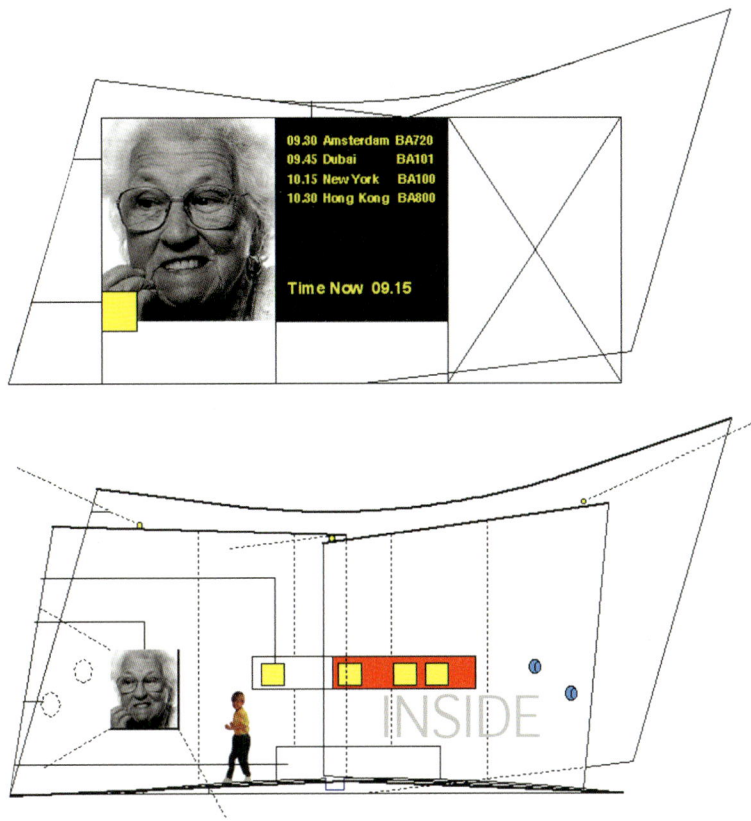

Proposal for an 'acoustic arch' to provide passenger information inside the Terminal 5 concourse at Heathrow Airport, London, 2000

clad structure. Our research identified that older travellers tended to use airport toilets frequently not simply because of a weak bladder but also because it was a calm, quiet place with good-quality sound for flight announcements.

BAA saw the potential in the 'sensory landscape' as a governing framework and proved amenable to many of the design ideas attached to it. The research team was asked to pilot key concepts in different parts of the existing Heathrow estate which were known to be unpopular with or troublesome to travellers. Tediously long walkways were covered with graphic panels showing fresh grass or autumn leaves, depending on the season. At points where passengers needed to make a decision where to go but frequently chose the wrong option, a visual balance between different options was promoted in the space using hanging textile banners. At the conclusion of the three-year intuitive navigation project at Terminal 5 in 2003, the BAA operations team was handed a set of wayfinding principles packaged in an interactive CD-Rom: these covered the whole range of passenger movement, from entrance and orientation to processing, decision point and exit.

DESIGNING A WORLD FOR EVERYONE

left
Design experiment inside the existing Heathrow Airport estate, with the use of hanging fabric banners to improve decision-making by passengers

below
Terminal 5 at Heathrow Airport today, with glowing autonomous structures punctuating the space

Terminal 5 at Heathrow opened five years later in 2008. Costing £4.2 billion and designed to handle 35 million passengers a year, it swiftly overcame the initial embarrassment of the failure of its baggage handling system to set a new, high-functioning benchmark for the regeneration of Heathrow Airport. Today, it remains the largest freestanding structure in the UK and its large expanses are punctuated by a series of autonomous micro-architectural elements – some more sensual than others – much in line with our recommendations. The acoustic arch, meanwhile, has become part of the architectural language of airports in many parts of the world; often it is branded by a perfume or tobacco company and serves coffee as well as information. If the original intent is sometimes diluted by the demands of airport marketing, it is a useful tool for people feeling lost and small in such noisy, cavernous spaces.

What you won't find at the heart of Heathrow Terminal 5 – or any other airport terminal for that matter – is a public swimming pool. The world is not ready for that yet. Nevertheless, the pool proposal served its purpose in shifting BAA's thinking on what a human-centred design approach might achieve in terms of being inclusive. And as a research centre, we learnt a valuable lesson in working with commercial partners that if you want to widen the field of creative opportunity, you should start right out on the margins of professional credibility.

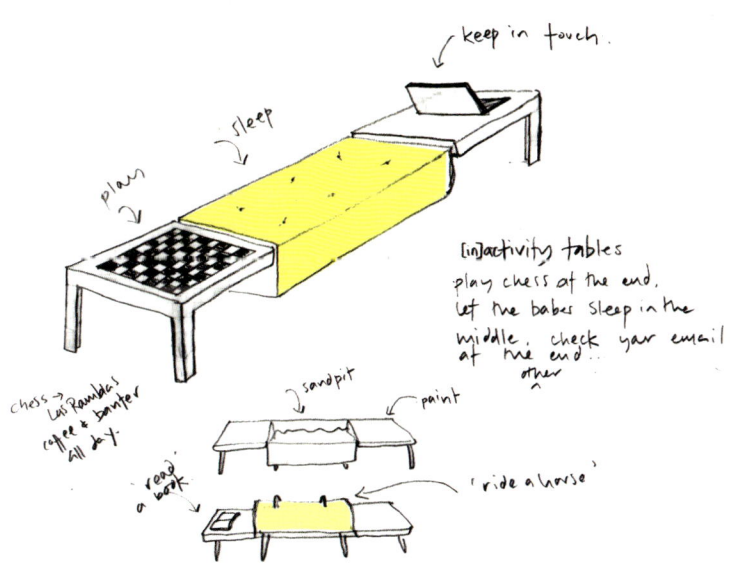

Sketch showing a proposal for over-sized furniture pieces in Terminal 5 at Heathrow Airport to relieve boredom and keep passengers occupied while waiting

Ambulance

The 'swoop and scoop' model of the emergency ambulance was first perfected by the British during the Crimean War (1853–1856). It is an approach that has been little altered since. By the start of the 21st century, ambulances were still rushing around our towns and cities scooping up patients and ferrying them in haste to busy, hard-pressed hospital Accident & Emergency departments, whatever their condition. But what if the ambulance interior could be redesigned to provide high-tech diagnostics on the move, and advanced care for patients in the community, without the familiar dash back to the hospital?

That was the question a research team at the Helen Hamlyn Centre for Design asked itself, in one of the largest multi-partner, multi-disciplinary development projects the centre has ever undertaken. Our study of the modern ambulance was actually three projects in one, and it spanned several years. It all began with a brief from the NHS National Patient Safety Agency, which made a safety risk assessment of a typical patient journey from emergency call to A&E unit following an appalling family tragedy in which a patient fell out of the back of an ambulance and was knocked over and killed by her own parents following in the car behind. The National Patient Safety Agency concluded that, when things went wrong, design factors were often responsible. This assessment came against the backdrop of an imminent planned reconfiguration of national ambulance services.

In response, an initial project – Designing Future Ambulance Transport for Patient Safety (2005–2006) – was set up to establish design requirements within the UK ambulance service and to identify obstacles to change. This work led to a second academic study – the Smart Pods Project (2007–2009) – which brought together research by clinicians, designers, social scientists, ergonomists and operational management analysts with one purpose: to propose innovative changes to the system that would reduce patient journeys and hospital admissions. The Smart Pods study estimated that up to 40 per cent of unnecessary patient journeys to A&E could be avoided by providing proper treatment inside the ambulance, thus reducing operational costs for the NHS.

The third and final part of the programme was a complete redesign of the current A&E ambulance interior (2010–2011). Building on the evidence base, this was developed by bringing together frontline paramedics, clinicians, patients, academic researchers, engineers and designers in a co-design process. It set out to create a new ambulance fit for 21st-century healthcare by addressing key design challenges identified in earlier phases of the work. These included: higher standards of hygiene and cleanliness; a less stressful patient experience; improved stock control, with modular treatment packs to make it easier for paramedics to restock the ambulance; better technology integration to receive and transmit patient data, with advanced digital diagnostics; reduced carbon footprint; interior reconfiguration to improve working processes; and future-proofing the design through modular componentry.

In order to understand the complexity of the ambulance service, our designers joined ambulance crews on several 12-hour ride-outs. The London Ambulance Service seconded an experienced emergency care practitioner to join the design team. Key insights were translated into sketch designs and a full-scale test rig simulating the treatment space was mocked up in cardboard and foam at the RCA. Groups of paramedics were then invited to evaluate a range of different proposals, using co-creation methods and focusing on key

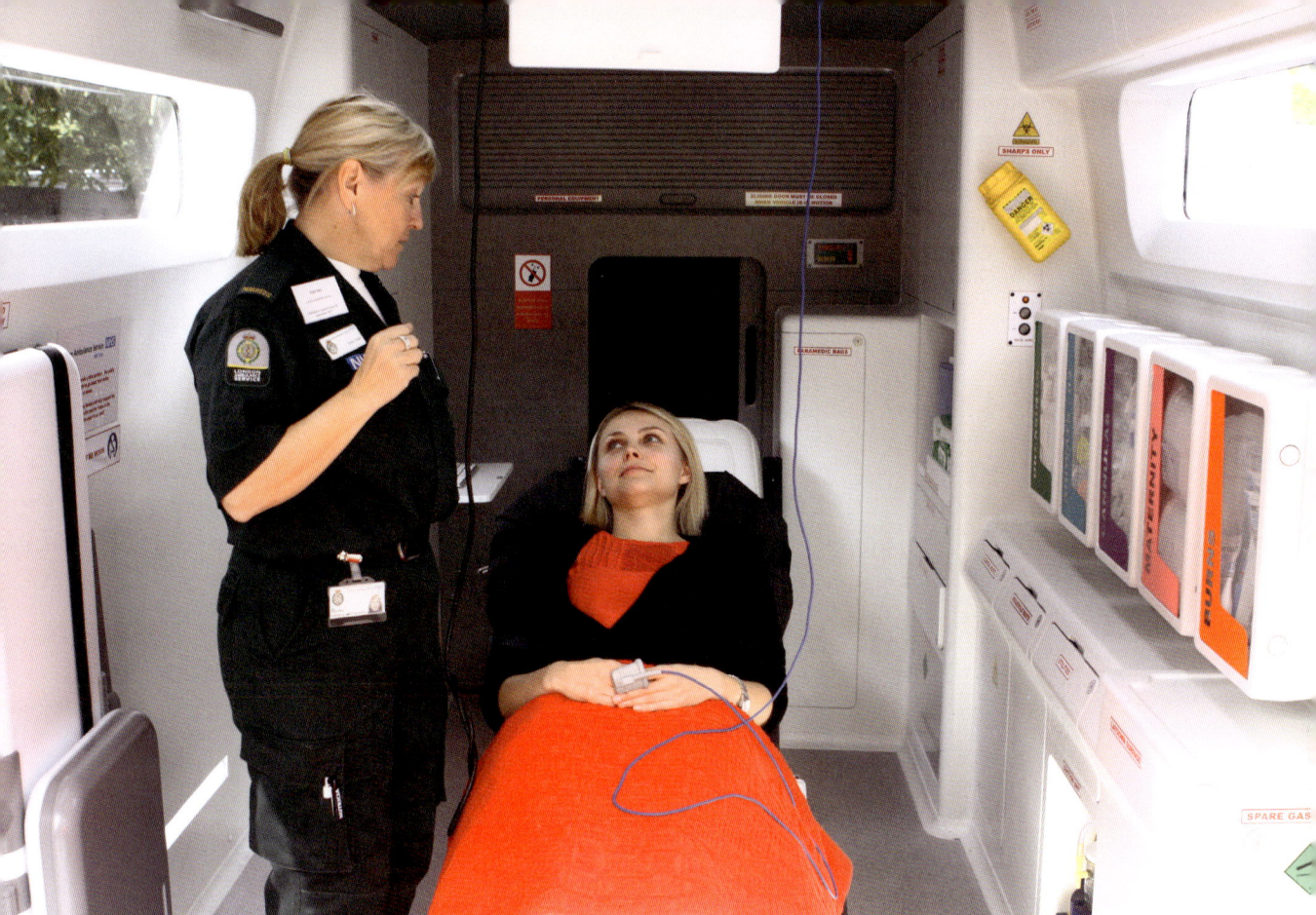

London Ambulance Service paramedic Dixie Dean, who was seconded to the RCA design team, reviews the new ambulance interior

opportunities for development. Gradually, a full-size mobile demonstrator took shape, fabricated from the shell of an old Australian ambulance bought on eBay for less than £500. The final hours of bidding for this vehicle without breaking the budget were among the most nerve-wracking moments of the entire project for the design team.

The new ambulance design features several innovations in the patient space: the stretcher is placed in the centre to give 360° access to the patient and to manage larger patients more easily; a simple-access working wall with fold-out table saves space; a new digital diagnostics and communications system gives better access to patient records; large skylights allow for more natural light inside the ambulance; consumables are reconfigured into modular treatment packs for specific emergencies (such as a burns or maternity pack); an easy-clean interior improves infection control, with curved plastic surfaces borrowed from studying yacht interiors; and staff are given hand-washing facilities and storage for belongings.

Clinical trials involving patient accident simulations showed that there was an improvement in paramedic performance inside the new interior compared to the existing ambulance. The problems faced by medical teams in cleaning, stocking and working in the emergency ambulance were addressed in such a creative way that the project received international acclaim. In 2012, it won the Transport category of the Design of the Year Awards given by the Design Museum and a

Interior of the new emergency ambulance with easy-clean surfaces, daylighting, modular treatment packs, a central stretcher and a jump-seat for a family member or friend to accompany the patient, 2011

Researchers Yusuf Muhammad (centre) and Gianpaolo Fusari at work inside a cardboard mock-up of the treatment space with paramedic Dixie Dean

Silver Award for Research in the IDEA awards run by the Industrial Designers Society of America. The ambulance was also exhibited in Vienna and New York.

In retrospect, that was the easy part. The final step was to commercialise the new design and this proved the hardest thing to do. Ambulance trusts and manufacturers took approving note of the various innovations that were presented and began to incorporate certain features in their own vehicles. But despite speaking to potential investors from Qatar to Russia, we were unable to find an industrial or healthcare partner to take the entire project forward into production entirely as we envisaged it. The leap from mobile demonstrator exhibited inside a Mercedes Sprinter box on the back of trailer to a fully working vehicle on the road proved a bridge too far.

One could argue that our new design simply ran too far ahead of the complete systems re-boot of ambulance services that would be required to make sense of the overall concept. If you introduce just-in-time modular treatment packs inside the ambulance (such as a burns pack for a fire emergency or a maternity pack for a pregnancy emergency), then a culture change is required in how London ambulances are restocked and paramedics are trained. If you envisage a scenario

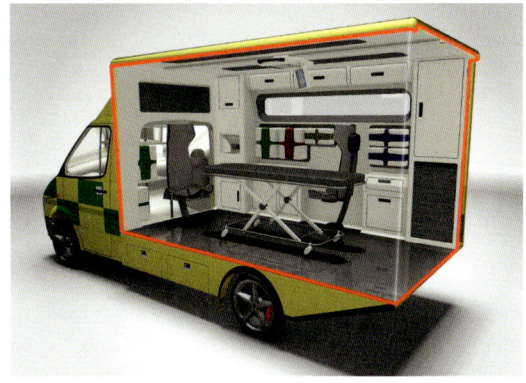

in which the ambulance crew can pull up on-screen patient records of the road crash victim that the ambulance is speeding towards, then those digital records need to be readily available.

Ultimately, we created a compelling vehicle design proposition that was out of step with the politically riven, fragmented, stop-start nature of the way ambulances are procured and specified in the UK. The emergency ambulance design continues to influence new practice in the field, however, and it remains one of the standout projects in 30 years of support by the Helen Hamlyn Trust for the RCA.

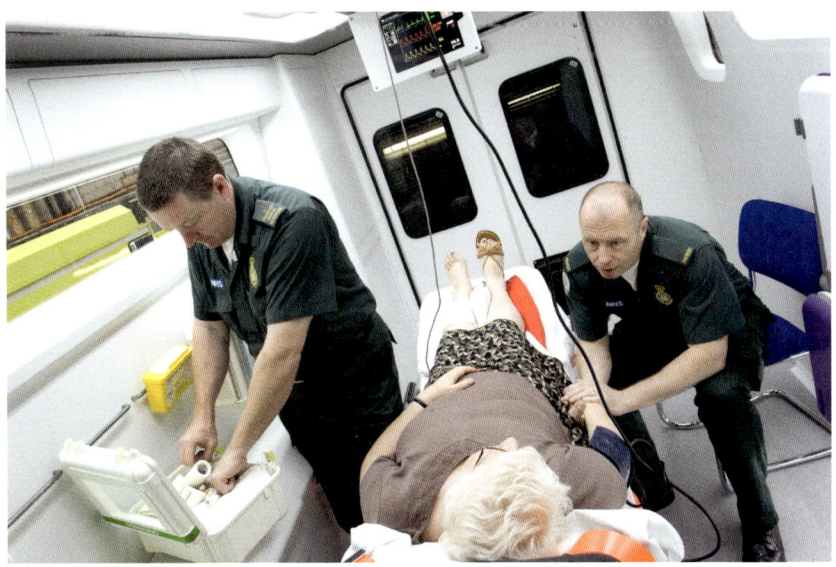

above

A cutaway computer model presents the key features of the new design

left

Paramedics conduct a clinical trial with a patient simulation inside the new ambulance, accessing the treatment packs and digital information system above

Bank

Across Europe, the high street bank branch has been a reassuring presence in our communities. But in the digital age, as more and more of us switch to online banking, they have been closing at an alarming rate. Many customers are happy to bank online without queues and at a time to suit them. But for some groups, especially older people, those with visual impairments and those without access to technology, online banking is not an option and branch closures represent the loss of a lifeline.

The banks themselves recognise what is lost in withdrawing from a physical high street presence to offer digital-only services: community engagement suffers and responding to customer needs becomes harder. On the other hand, the economic case for keeping large, single-use bank branches open no longer makes sense given reduced footfall. But what if a high street bank could adopt a hybrid retail approach? What if it could combine banking services with other customer-facing facilities such as bookshops, cafes, restaurants or co-working spaces, thus spreading the cost of branch location? What if a new strategy could merge physical and digital space?

These were the questions we asked when the Helen Hamlyn Centre for Design undertook a project in 2016 with UniCredit, an Italian banking and financial services company that operates globally. This bank wanted to get closer to the communities it serves, make better use of its large and empty banking halls, and create a more effective working environment for its staff. The study began with a tour of hybrid spaces in London and Milan and a mapping of their common elements. Co-creation workshops were held with UniCredit employees and customers to establish a framework of user needs. The project then developed an architectural 'kit of parts' to aid the flexible re-purposing of UniCredit's bank branches for more hybrid uses.

At the centre of this modular design approach was a service bar – common to retail, hospitality, work and banking spaces – which became the main activation device for each scheme. The service bar acted as a 'blade' to penetrate each hybrid space, referencing the rituals of retail environments while offering a new and innovative service approach. Critically, it provided the primary point around which a flexible, modular architectural structure could be built within any given volume. We then introduced digital services to enhance the interactions between people and place, improving access for vulnerable customers. This was based on four levels of interaction, from free wi-fi right up to location-based media and augmented environments.

In the final stages of the project, we combined the architectural components, digital layer and people-centred aspects of the project to create three models of the future hybrid bank branch, each at a different scale. The Mini Hybrid model is still recognisably a bank branch. It gives up to 90 per cent of the space to banking. The bank owns the space and gets a small cost contribution from other partners such as a bookshop in the corner or a coffee shop area.

The Midi Hybrid model devotes only around 50 per cent of space to banking services. The bank still owns the space, but a large proportion of the costs are reimbursed by external partners such as flexible workspace providers who might operate and manage this new model as a joint venture, with a growing focus on building membership as part of an enhanced customer experience. The Maxi Hybrid model devotes only ten per cent of the space to banking services. There is a diverse mix of retail stores, exhibition areas and interactive zones. This model is about shared ownership and increasing customer coverage in a less intensive

Mini Hybrid bank branch concept with space for co-working in the foreground

and more interesting way; the hybrid space is not perceived as a bank branch anymore but as a new, mixed-use environment.

Two scenarios were developed – one on a coastal site and one in a city centre – to show how the new strategy could play out in different settings. In July 2017, UniCredit converted a former traditional bank branch in Via Verdi, Milan, into a Mini Hybrid business centre combining co-working, meeting and event spaces. This marked the first physical implementation of the research, encouraging the Italian banking giant to delve deeper into the potential of hybrid place-making as a solution to the disappearing bank branch.

right
First UniCredit hybrid bank branch opened in Via Verdi, Milan, 2017

Midi Hybrid bank branch concept, with only half of the space devoted to banking services

Maxi Hybrid bank branch concept with banking services integrated discreetly into a large mixed-use environment

above
Illustrations for scenarios showing a hybrid bank branch in use

Bathroom

Better bathroom design can often be the difference between whether an older person remains in their own home or whether they are forced into institutionalised care. Bathing is one of the main activities of daily living on which any assessment of the ability to live independently is made. But in the necessary drive to ensure that there is a safe and sterile environment with grab rails and anti-slip materials, bathrooms too often neglect the more sensory and indulgent aspects of bathing that bring pleasure and enjoyment to people. Everyone loves a bit of pampering. Taking pride in one's appearance does not diminish with advancing age.

One of the central themes of the Helen Hamlyn Centre for Design's work in this area has been to explore ways to go beyond a safety-first design approach in bathroom design to incorporate new ideas around sensuality, indulgence and delight. In 2006, for example, we began working with sanitary-ware manufacturer Ideal Standard to create a mirror and washbasin combination based on ethnographic research conducted with a group of older dancers and actresses, who have a professional interest in appearance and beauty, and could be described as 'expert users'.

Observations of their behaviour led to a new design with a series of floating, glowing and flexible elements – a departure in style from standard bathroom fittings. The basin floats away from the wall, and the main mirror incorporates a soft, glowing band of light that washes gently across the face. A handheld mirror detaches to allow the back and side of the head to be seen, while an adjustable tap allows users to wash their hair in the basin. The project's focus on sensuality and delight claims the bathroom as a place for grooming and pampering, whatever the age. Ideal Standard introduced the product at its annual press launch, having tested the water earlier in a more speculative project with our research team, entitled 'Indulgent Bathing'.

This formative study interviewed and photographed ten people aged 50–70 across a span of gender, ethnicity, social background and physical ability. The individual stories of these research participants were captured in a series of design concepts for Ideal Standard that took a more lyrical approach to the bathroom. One concept adopted the metaphor of the garden hose and people's love of gardening to create a nature-inspired network of hoses with changeable heads to stream water or hot air or create suction. Another applied the same principles around a freestanding tree-shaped unit complete with branches that turned into showerheads or served as seat supports.

A 'waterfall' proposal for a wet room transformed the floors, walls and ceilings of the bathroom into a rich, organic surface. Rolling, sensuous curves formed washbasins, bathing areas and storage space, prompting Ideal Standard's engineers to scratch their heads about how such designs might work within the constraints of British plumbing. Such ground-breaking work, however, did much to reinforce the idea of bathing as a form of therapy for older people – and a number of our other bathroom projects sought to overcome obstacles to successful, stress-free bathing.

A project with German shower manufacturer Hansgrohe looked at why so many older people preferred a bath to the therapeutic benefits of showering. This study concluded that lack of safety and comfort in the shower was a concern. A series of design concepts were developed to address these fears and included pressure-sensor tap tiles mounted into the ceramic surround and shower seating made from a continuous prefabricated ribbon.

We also worked with ESL Industries to design an accessible bath for older and frail people that

BATHROOM

Mirror-and-basin combination for Ideal Standard designed by Tomek Rygalik, 2007

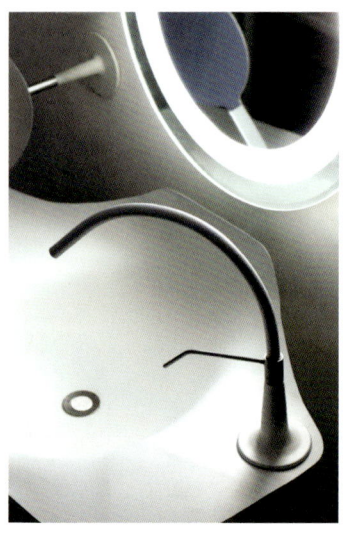

left
Tomek Rygalik's design was based on ethnographic study of older performers preparing to go on stage

below
'Waterfall' wet room: concept for Ideal Standard designed by Julie Mathias, 2005

right
Bringing the garden hose indoors: concept for Ideal Standard designed by Julie Mathias, 2005

BATHROOM

DESIGNING A WORLD FOR EVERYONE

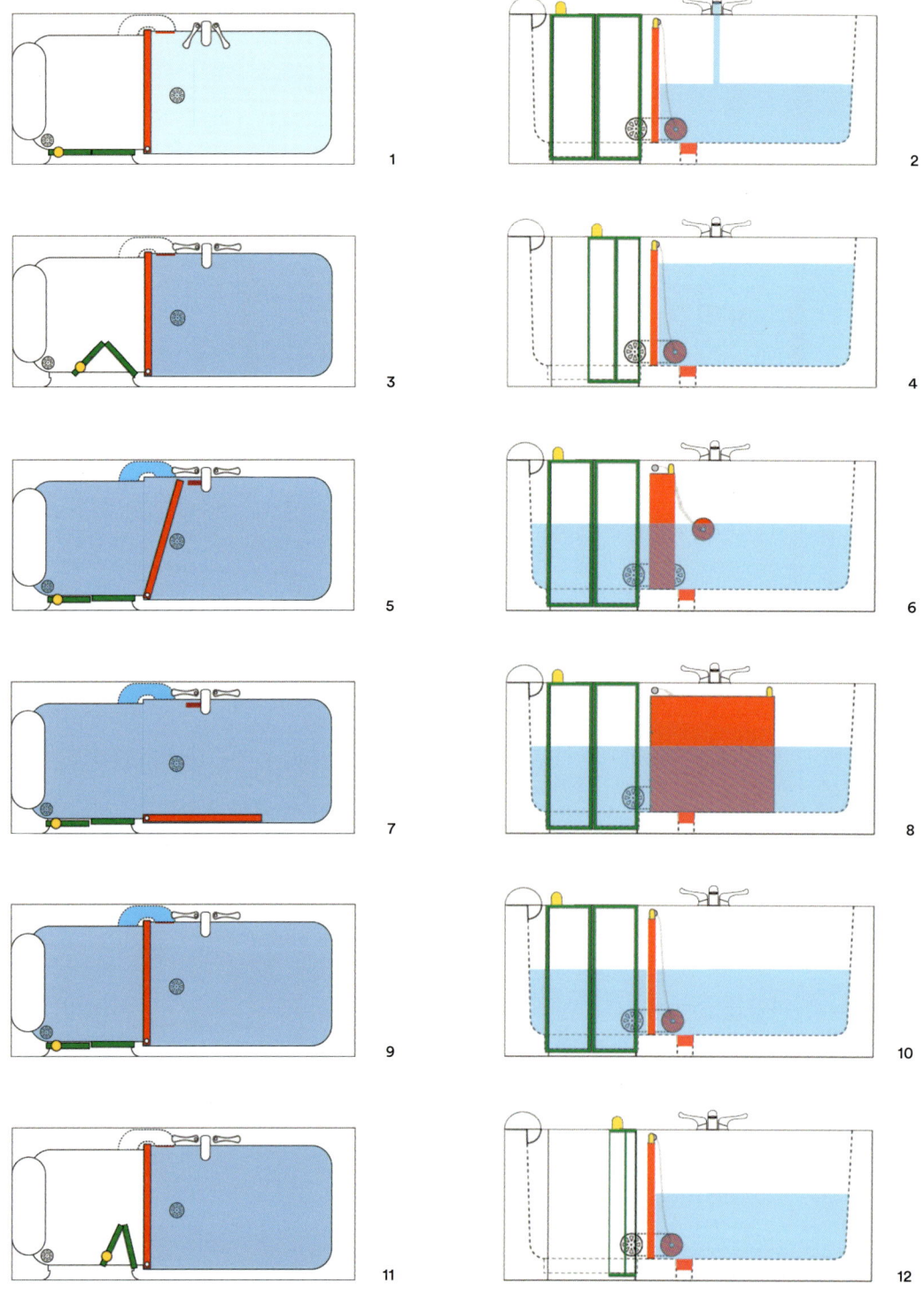

Diagrams illustrating the Watergate accessible bath design by Barnaby Barford for ELS Industries, 2003

left

Safer showering concept with wetroom for Hansgrohe designed by Mary Wagstaff, 2003

below

User research: older people often struggle when getting into a bath

looked attractive and did not scream 'special needs'. User research with carers and residents led to a new, prototype product called Watergate. The bath is divided by a pair of inner doors into two sections – a 'seated' area and a 'wet' area. Each section has its own plughole for drainage. The bath is accessed in four simple stages. First, the bather fills up the wet section of the bath prior to entry, checking the water is at the required temperature. Second, the bather enters the dry, seated section of the bath through level-access folding doors on the side of the bath, shuts the folding doors and sits down.

Third, the bather releases a simple mechanism which allows the pre-run water in the wet section of the bath to quickly flow into the seated area through a large-diameter tube. The bather is immediately immersed in warm water at the right temperature. Fourth, when the two water levels are at the same height, the inner doors are lightly pushed to float open and fold away into the side of the bath, creating a normal full-length bath in which the bather can choose whether to remain seated or move to a reclining position within the bath.

It was important that Watergate's inclusive design should be mainstream in appearance and able to fit in a normal-sized bathroom. A stigmatising experience does nothing to enhance the more health-inducing, indulgent dimension of bathing – and it is worth noting that in the years since these projects, the bathroom industry has done much to adopt a more inclusive approach based on sensuality and not just safety.

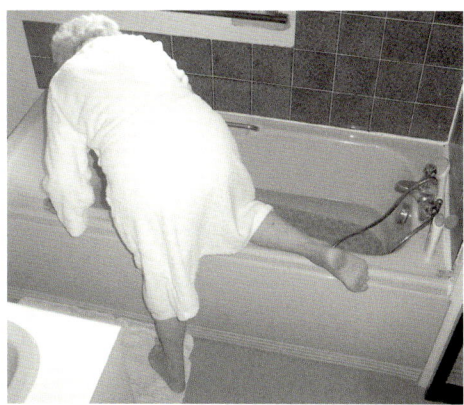

Beer Glass

It is a frustrating and familiar cycle of violence played out each weekend in Britain's pubs, clubs and bars. Inebriated young men fight one other, using beer glasses as weapons to inflict terrible facial injuries and scarring the night-time experience across our towns and cities. Glassing incidents are among the most severe manifestations of alcohol-related disorder. They cause terrible damage to the eye and face, usually require stitches or surgery, and can result in sight loss.

By 2009, there were 5,500 glassings reported annually – more than 100 per week. Overall, alcohol-related harm was costing the National Health Service an estimated £2.7 billion. Things felt out of control. Prompted by a Welsh facial reconstruction surgeon and criminologist, Jonathan

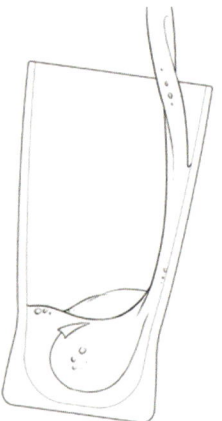

left

Design concept by Design Bridge for an unbreakable beer glass, with resin poured into the cavity between two thin walls, 2010

right, top

Design concept shows a beer glass with a plastic inner coating to prevent shards escaping on impact

right, bottom

Prototype beer glass with a 'twin wall' concept

Shepherd, who saw the impact of the problem right at the sharp end, the UK government decided to act. A partnership between the Home Office's Design and Technology Alliance Against Crime and the Design Council looked at whether the British pint glass – that symbol of our national life – could be redesigned to make it shatterproof and safe.

Our research team at the RCA led a project codenamed SWIG (Safe Ways In Glass) to explore the issue with drinkers, pub owners, police, licensee officers, plastic surgeons and the drinks industry. This study revealed limitations in the two main alternatives to annealed glass (from which pint glasses are conventionally made): toughened glass is expensive and has a tendency to shatter spontaneously; plastic glasses such as those made of polycarbonate, while much safer, are generally disliked by drinkers.

A design team from Design Bridge, a consulting firm with extensive experience in drinks branding, joined the project. Four routes for development were identified: a 'hybrid' solution making plastic feel more like glass; an 'ultimate toughened glass' which solves the shatter problem; a 'glass-plus' idea in which the inside wall of the vessel is sprayed with a thin plastic coating to stop any shards escaping on impact; and a 'twin wall' concept derived from the car windscreen industry in which a bio-based resin sits between two thin walls that comprise the glass. This last route was seen as having the most consumer appeal and commercial potential.

The concepts were prototyped with a manufacturing partner, Arc International, and piloted in UK pub chains. The entire project was formally launched by Home Secretary Alan Johnson in February 2010 and featured on ITV's morning programme, 'Daybreak', where guests on the sofa tried and failed to smash the new pint glass. Never has a project left me with such mixed emotions – the pleasure of downing a pint for strictly professional reasons and the pain of studying the details of facial reconstruction surgery where the pint glass has become a weapon.

Bus Stop

For many people who are visually impaired, elderly or have mobility difficulties, the bus may be their only means of independent and affordable travel. Could a redesign of the bus stop create a more accessible environment and improve communication between the bus driver and passengers with diverse needs? We worked with design firm Lacock Gullam to investigate the considerable challenges that people face when boarding a bus. Is the waiting area safe? Can we identify that it is the right bus? Will the driver admit wheelchair users? Is the bus information reliable?

The solution incorporated existing technologies into a reconfigured bus shelter. A bus shelter typically contains service-related information, with advertising panels to finance its maintenance, but their location creates a visual and physical obstruction to linear movement along the pavement. By off-setting the ad panel from the waiting area and turning it to face the road, all information,

Reconfigured bus shelter by Lacock Gullam creates a more inclusive experience, 2004

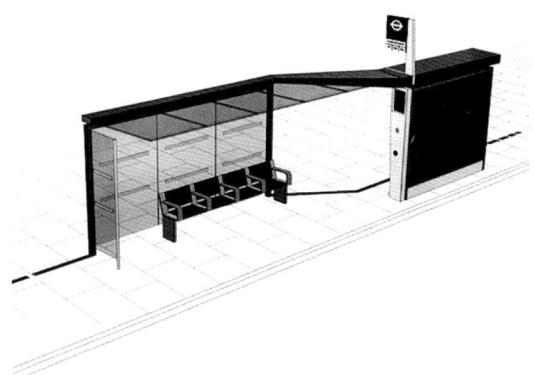

Freed of all other functions, this light, open, yet protected waiting area improves the bus driver's ability to understand the situation at the bus stop and manage passenger flow on and off the bus. The backbone of the roof that connects the two areas of the shelter can be equipped with lighting, speakers and CCTV, enhancing safety.

As well as the bus network becoming more accessible, the shelter acts as a landmark for visually impaired people: audio announcements of arriving buses are activated by a device in their ticket wallet. Lacock Gullam's bus stop was a winning entry in the 2004 DBA (Design Business Association) Inclusive Design Challenge, run by the Helen Hamlyn Centre for Design.

ticketing, mapping and timetable requirements can be contained behind the advertising surface, with a dedicated area for help points, journey planners and web-based screen facilities.

Creating a well-lit and standardised display area makes the information more legible and accessible. The roof of this area is just wide enough for protection from the weather but discourages its use as a waiting area, affording a clearer view of approaching buses. The roof widens over the waiting area to the full width of the shelter, creating better wheelchair access. Generous seats with contrasting armrests provide greater comfort yet leave free space for wheelchair users to be at the best possible location for accessing the bus.

Care Home

Planning the future care home: Helen Hamlyn design researcher Gregor Timlin (second right) leads a research workshop with UK provider Bupa

CARE HOME

The care home environment is one of the most complex and challenging for designers because it must cater for the widest range of age-related impairments among residents within one space. This span of abilities has been termed 'from agile to fragile' as service providers struggle to cope with the conflicting priorities of different physical and cognitive needs. Although levels of mobility tend to vary, typically, 70 per cent of care home residents exhibit significant confusion and other cognitive impairments such as dementia.

Our design research in this highly demanding area has ranged from large-scale site layouts of new homes to the details and furnishing of individual rooms and the design of individual artefacts used as part of care. At the core of our work has been a desire to create spaces that feel more like a 'home', restore a sense of dignity and individual self-worth, compensate for multiple disabilities and help older residents to remain active for longer.

A research programme in the UK with Bupa Care Homes engaged staff, residents, relatives and experts in an immersive process. This led to new layout proposals and to the development of a range of new products to improve the resident experience of dining rooms and bedrooms; these included new furniture, lighting and tableware to assist eating and drinking in a more dignified way and to compensate for poor vision and dexterity.

Families objected to their elderly relatives drinking from cheap, plastic children's cups, for example, so we created more attractive ceramic beakers to replace them. In the bedroom, a modular new wardrobe, dresser and customisable room layout was created using rail and hook display techniques from the retail sector; inside the wardrobe, a new hanger design allowed care stuff to lay out an entire outfit for residents to dress themselves without assistance.

right, top
New tableware for assisted dining designed by Gregor Timlin for Bupa, 2009

right, bottom
Ceramic beaker: a more dignified solution for care home residents

Bedroom furniture designed by Nick Rysenbry for Bupa, 2009

In Hong Kong and Scandinavia, we brought the same participatory, human-centric approach to entirely different cultural contexts. Research in care homes in Denmark, Sweden and Norway led to a series of new care furniture pieces on the theme of 'togetherness', in recognition of the need for psychological support as well as ergonomic comfort. These prototypes included a 'conversation chair' with a large sound-proofed shell for people who are hard of hearing.

The Hong Kong study was called 'Ageing in a Vertical City'. Our research team visited five care homes in Hong Kong high-rise blocks, as well as older people still living independently, to gain first-hand experience of cramped living conditions. The project resulted in a series of proposals including a new bed space design that offered more functionality in terms of providing care, creating privacy, organising storage and connecting to the outside world through digital projection. The results of the study were given a public exhibition in Hong Kong as part of a growing global debate about how we can redesign care homes to be safer and better.

Care homes have received relatively little design attention compared to other environments. The spotlight thrown on the vulnerability of care home residents by the global Coronavirus pandemic of 2020 suggests that we will be seeing a lot more focus on innovation in the future.

CARE HOME

Full-size prototype and sketch for conversation chair designed by Lisa Johansson, 2014

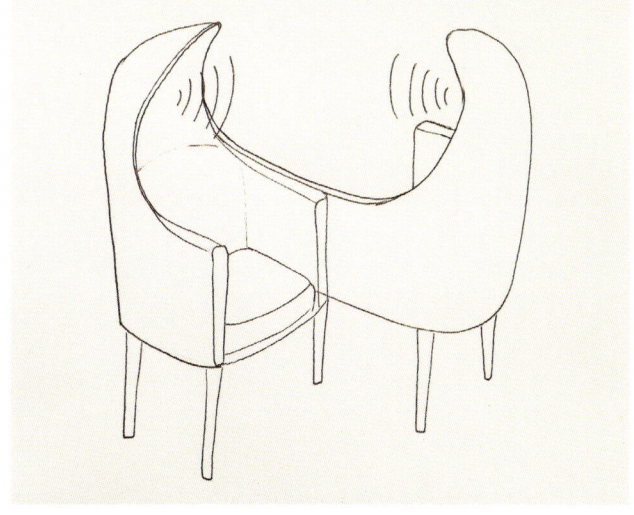

Prototype bed space for the Hong Kong 'Ageing in a Vertical City' project, 2017

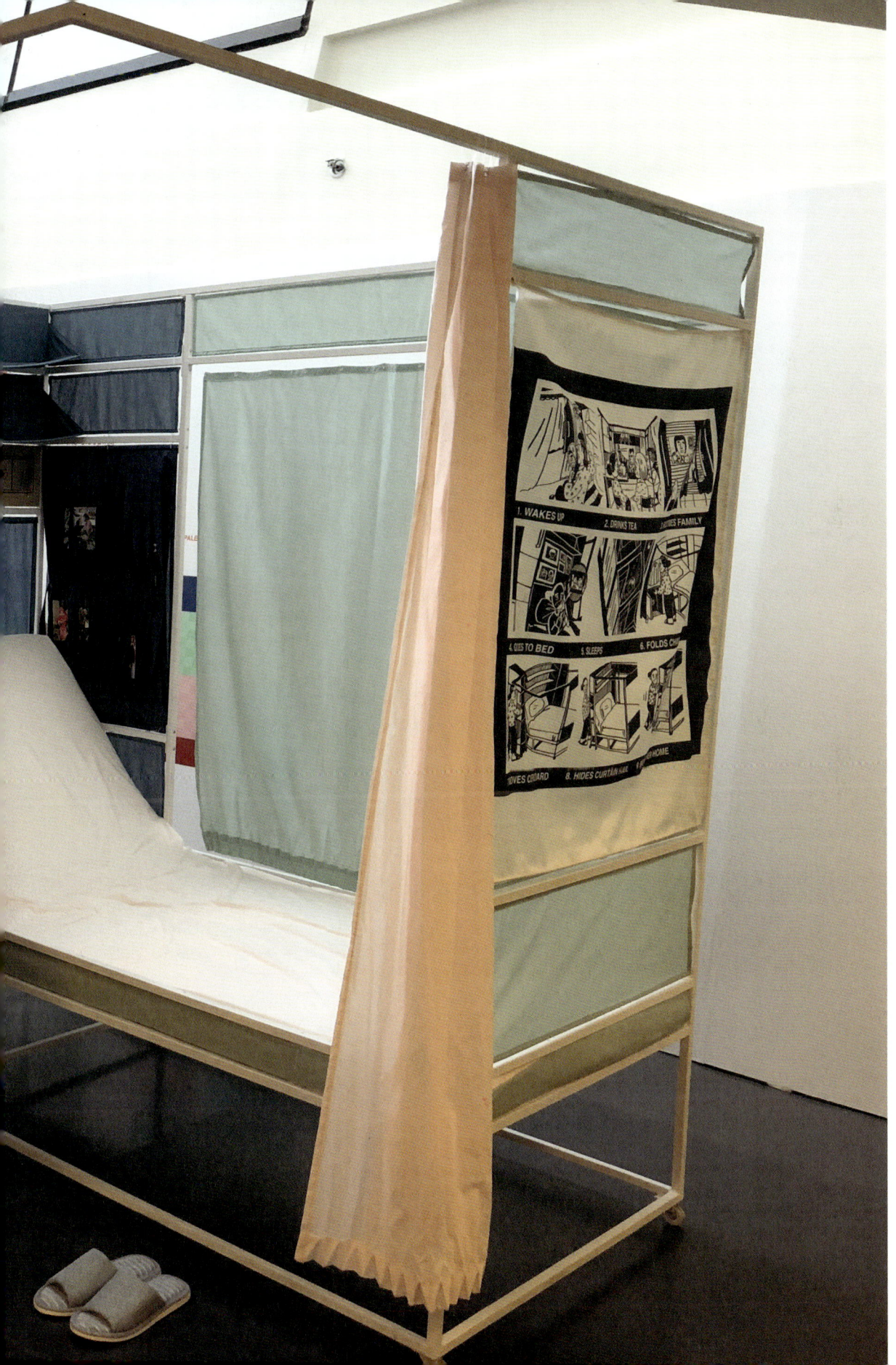

Classroom

above

Test-rig in a London classroom reconfigures fluorescent lights for more focus on activities. Project by Amanda Buckley, 2014

left

Experiment with artificial lighting in a London classroom evaluated for its effect

How can the design of the school classroom support learning and aid concentration by pupils? We looked at this issue from a range of angles and identified that one of the biggest factors in maintaining mood and motivation during lessons among secondary school pupils is how the classroom is lit. Over the past 50 years there have been enormous changes in how pupils aged 11–17 are taught and how they learn. But one thing that hasn't changed is the artificial lighting of the learning environment, despite the widespread adoption of new communication technologies – from digital whiteboards to laptops and projectors – as part of the education process.

To investigate sustainable and effective ways to light the secondary school classroom, we set up a two-year project of in-depth research conducted in London, Hong Kong and Trondheim, Norway. We examined different environmental conditions, from the short, dark winter days in Scandinavia to the long, bright, summer ones in China. A series of classroom workshops, test-rigs and visual experiments explored ways to balance natural and electric lighting, support group learning and address the visual discomfort that can arise from a mismatch between lighting and the IT technologies now widely used in schools.

What we learnt was that lighting has a profound impact on behaviour, motivation and wellbeing among adolescent learners, but those running secondary schools do not know enough about the subject. As a result, most classrooms are lit in an indiscriminate and inflexible way. So, we published a guide for school leaders, entitled *Switched On*, to illuminate the subject.

School bag that doubles as a seat cushion designed by Mark Champkins, 2003

At the other end of the spectrum, we looked at concentration levels among fidgety primary school pupils, reaching different conclusions about the likely causes. Research in five London primary school classrooms revealed that dehydration and lack of comfort caused younger pupils to lose focus. A series of design proposals were created to enhance concentration. Two of them were prototyped and taken back to the classroom for user testing, as part of a broader objective to engage teachers more directly in a design dialogue: a water bottle that doubles as a pencil holder and pencil sharpener, encouraging pupils to drink sufficiently; and a school bag that doubles as a seat cushion when slung over the chair back, making the chair less uncomfortable.

Primary school pupil with a seat cushion and a water bottle holding a pencil

Crutch

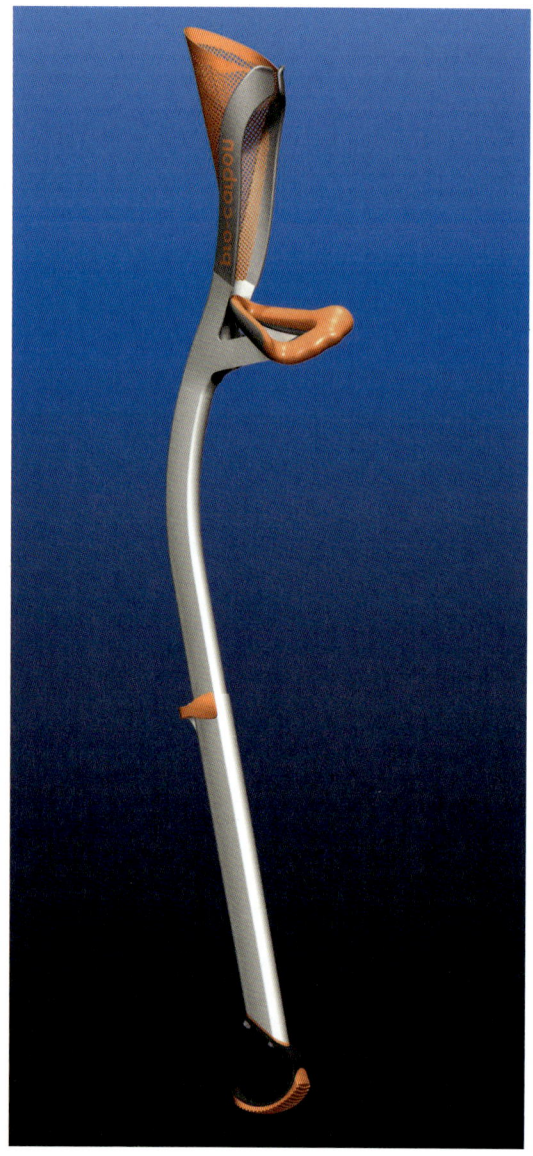

For many people in the UK, the standard National Health Service crutch is unfit for purpose. A key problem is that its narrow handles cut into the soft part of the hand during use, causing discomfort. Hospitals spend millions each year handing out crutches, walking sticks and wheelchairs to patients who break or discard them. Four out of five walking aids are never returned. Between 2016 and 2019, the cost to the NHS was more than £14 million.

RCA industrial design engineering graduate Guy Robinson discovered the drawbacks of traditional crutches when he was forced to hobble around on them after a serious car accident damaged his knee. He found the crutches unwieldy; they hurt rather than helped. So, he decided to develop his own state-of-the-art version, which became the focus of a project developed in the Helen Hamlyn Centre for Design and supported by the Audi Design Foundation.

The direction taken was to redefine the walking aid as professional sports equipment. The aim was to replace the old approach of one-size-fits-all with a new level of customisation, comfort and performance. Robinson designed new carbon-fibre crutches, called Pro Crutches, as series of separate, interchangeable components that are assembled to best fit an individual's body, ability and style.

Carbon fibre was chosen as it is easy enough to mould but strong enough to provide support, redistributing pressure away from the soft middle part of the hand. A spring-like foot was designed at the base of the crutch which cushions the impact at the start of the step – an idea derived from studying the design of prosthetics.

Standard NHS crutch redesigned as an item of professional sports equipment by Guy Robinson, 2002

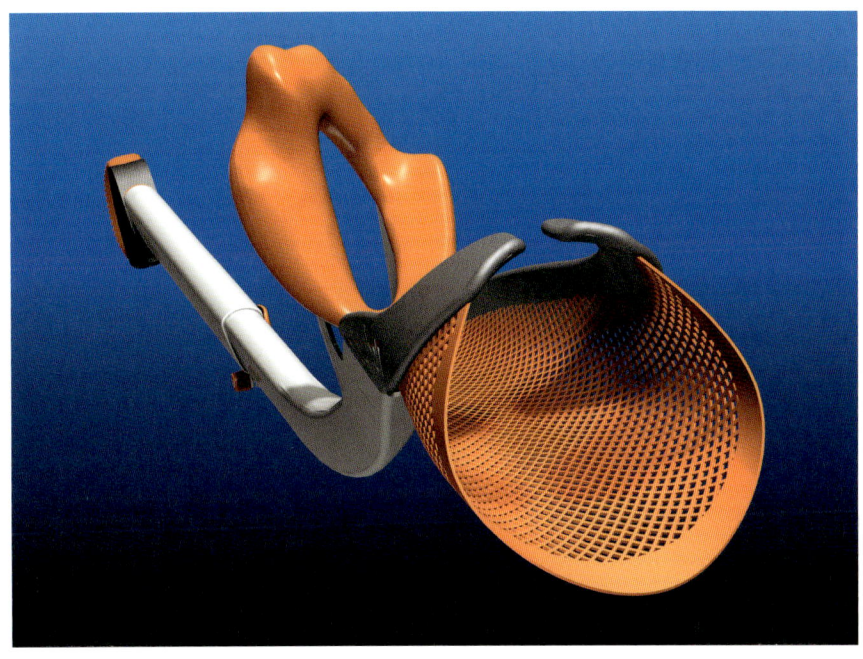

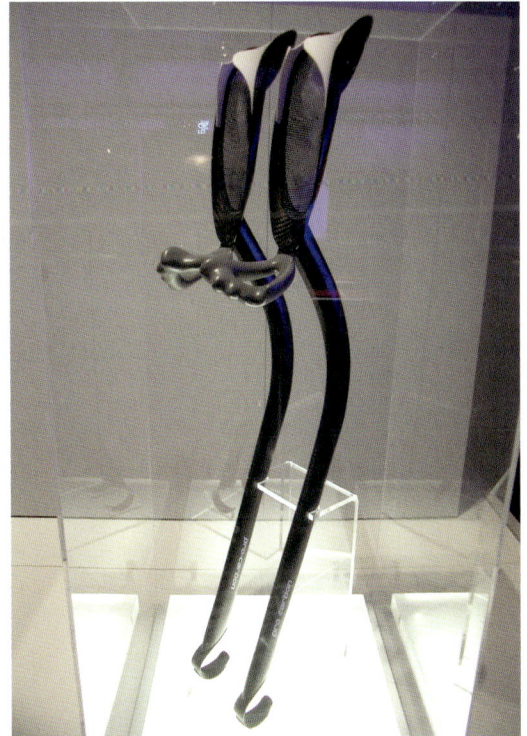

right
Carbon-fibre Pro Crutches on display at the Science Museum, London

The Pro Crutches design won several awards, was exhibited at the Science Museum in London, and was featured on the BBC. It never replaced the standard NHS crutch as the cost of carbon-fibre production could not compete with the lower unit cost of the existing product. Nevertheless, it opened a debate about cost and value in NHS procurement. The problem of low-quality crutches has not gone away. If people saw the crutch as a professional piece of sports rehabilitation equipment, might they perhaps treat them with more respect, return and reuse them, and save costs to the NHS over time?

Desk

Our interest in designing the desk is a direct result of a long-term research focus by the Helen Hamlyn Centre for Design on working from home. Given the massive swing towards home-working in the early 2020s, we can say we were clearly ahead of the curve. One of our first public events as a research centre in the late 1990s was called 'Work At Home', a symposium preceded by an ethnographic study of home-workers.

This study identified four models based on the 'borders' that people construct to protect and enable work within the home. Two were successful models of working at home; two were unsuccessful. The first we called the Contained Work model, where the borders constructed around work are solid, allowing little that doesn't belong to pass in or out, and clearly defining the parameters of work within the home. Spatial borders are marked with a separate room or a garden shed perhaps; temporal borders are defined. Psychologically, the distinction between home and work is clear in the worker's mind.

Sitting on the opposite end of an axis in terms of the degree of separation of work from home was the Permeable Work model. Here, the borders are constructed to allow a planned integration of work and home activities and easy two-directional access. Domestic and work activities are intertwined or run in parallel, often in the same space. The other two models demonstrated conditions where borders were not successfully constructed or maintained. In the Overflowing Work model, work has burst its banks and flooded the home. The work is not contained by spatial or temporal borders, it cannot be shut or folded away, and the worker is constantly investing more and more time in the work and neglecting other basic functions of home life.

Its counterpart is the Imploding Work model where resources are drained or channelled away from work, and less and less work is achieved. Workspace dissolves – psychologically and practically; plans disintegrate; motivation and discipline weaken in the face of competing demands and constant interruptions and diversions (visitors, babies, builders, depression).

These four models were fleshed out with scenarios, sketch designs and prototypes to show how borders might be created between work and home. This line of thinking was extended to follow-on projects, including a range of production-ready home office furniture called Envelope which responds to the scenario of permeable borders. The desk is designed to sit easily in a domestic living room, its split-level form indicating the idea of a contained work zone. An inner light is activated by lifting your pen from a groove to symbolise the ritual of starting work.

We also worked with the disability charity Leonard Cheshire in 2000 to develop new furniture for wheelchair-using home-workers, who experience above-average levels of unemployment due to lack of access to the workplace. Among the design proposals to emerge from the research was a horseshoe-shaped desk designed to give wheelchair users the maximum work area from one single point, and with a turntable beneath to simulate the movement of a swivelling office chair when the wheelchair is driven onto its platform.

Many years later, when I curated an exhibition called *New Old* for the Design Museum, a special design commission returned to the design of the desk for home-working. Munich-based designer Konstantin Grcic, an RCA graduate, was invited to develop a proposal which explored the relationship between older people and the working world. He designed an outdoor structure for working called

Envelope home office desk designed by Peter Fullager and Dan Jones, 2004

left
Desk created for the disability charity Leonard Cheshire by Lotta Vaanenen, 2000

right
Groove detail preventing small objects from rolling off the surface

Head in the Sky: a safe place for concentration for those who are still living life to the full. The mesh structure is open at the top to give thoughts free rein but is constrained by verticals along the sides. This notion of envelopment and enclosure was inspired by Antonello da Messina's painting *Saint Jerome in his Study* from 1475. The design creates the outline of a table, a seat and a shelf within a limited area. A ramp attached to the design alludes to disability but instead appears to symbolise a new beginning for older workers. The proposal is loaded with symbolism but also offers a practical solution as more and more of us are set to work from home for longer.

Head in the Sky outdoor workspace designed by Konstain Grcic, 2017

Food Pack

If there is one barrier to daily living that older people complain about more than any other, it is the difficulty in opening food packaging. Consumer reports over many years have repeatedly highlighted the issue – and we've been determined to find ways to address it as a research centre. One of our very first high-profile business collaborations, in 1994, was with Rockware Glass and the Safeway supermarket chain to develop a glass jar that older and disabled people could open without recourse to an adaptive device or the intervention of a strongman neighbour.

The solution, designed by RCA ceramics and glass student Gavin Pryke, was a new jar shape with a square lid that was easier for people of all ages to grasp, twist and open. Our partners saw the commercial potential in such a simple but effective idea, and the project went on to address storage, labelling and product presentation. Early success with one supermarket chain didn't make the problem go away, however. In 2002, we began working with Waitrose supermarkets after one of our research team took photographs of his grandmother struggling with the chain's own-brand packaging and we sent them to the Waitrose board.

The Waitrose project studied in depth how older customers opened (or failed to open) food packs. It created an improvement strategy for the company to make its packaging more age-friendly, alongside some fast-track minor changes that could deliver major benefits with minimal disruption to supply chains. Five of the most problematic pack types were redesigned with simple adjustments: bacon packs, fresh soup pots, ring-pull cans, jam jars and sardine tins. We went on to work with Marks & Spencer, using video ethnography techniques to observe how four UK

A Jar We Can Open by Gavin Pryke, 1994: the square top was developed by Rockware Glass and the Safeway supermarket chain

left, top
Redesign of the ring-pull on Waitrose canned goods, 2002

left, bottom
Making the Waitrose bacon pack easier to open, 2002

right
Milkman by Factory Design: a concept to redesign the milk carton for people with arthritis, 2000

households shop and prepare meals. This project produced a set of exemplar pack designs, as well as a practical design tool to guide company development of better packaging.

One product line not on the shopping list, however, was the standard milk carton, an item that can be immensely frustrating to open for people with reduced grip. To find a more inclusive solution, we collaborated with a creative team at Factory Design and a group of people with severe arthritis to develop a concept called Milkman. The solution was inspired in part by the garden hose, where kinks will cut off water flow. The spout of the container could work in the same way – when it is down, it pinches and the fluid is sealed; when it is up and open, the milk can flow out. The new carton was also given grip detail using rubberised ink on its sides for easier handling.

Packaging continues to prove a thorn in the side for many people. The less acceptable it is to have chemical preservatives in food, the more packaging itself is called upon to do the preserving, and the harder packs become to open. But at least the packaging industry can't say there aren't lots of tested, easy-to-open design solutions available.

Garden

Concept sketch for the garden at Kingwood College, with a range of different spaces that address the needs and interests of adults with autism

For most of us, residential gardens provide an entirely familiar, reassuring and enjoyable experience. The restorative qualities of gardens and the benefits of interacting with nature are widely documented. But for some people with autism, the garden can be a terrifying place. The dynamic and unpredictable nature of the great outdoors, with falling leaves, shifting light and shade, changing weather and seasons, presents a challenge for those whose sensory sensitivities can

require a constant and never-changing routine. As a result, they are sometimes too anxious to venture outdoors and are denied the therapeutic benefits of gardens and gardening.

So, how could we make the garden more accessible for autistic adults with sensory differences? That question formed part of a major research programme in partnership with a charity, the Kingwood Trust. The work was conducted by Katie Gaudion, the first successful PhD candidate in the history of the Helen Hamlyn Centre for Design, and focused on designing for the sensory preferences and special interests of adults with autism living in sheltered accommodation provided by Kingwood.

Through a co-design process with autistic residents, care staff and relatives, the study generated a set of guidelines for designing a sensory garden based around sight, touch, smell, sound, movement and perception. Flexible design principles covered a range of issues from planting to pathways, catering for people with autism who are both hyper-sensitive (avoiding sensory stimulation) and hypo-sensitive (seeking it). At Kingwood College, these principles were put into practice with the design and construction of a large new garden.

This garden contains several important features including transition space to allow for a gradual acclimatisation to outdoors, escape space for people to hide away in secluded areas, exercise space to improve mood and wellbeing, and wilderness space for exploration. There are also areas for special interests such as horticulture, for social interaction with others, and for specific sensory experiences – all part of an inclusive approach to opening up green outdoor space for the enjoyment of people with autism.

left
A Kingwood resident enjoys potting plants in the Kingwood College garden: activities are geared to different sensory preferences

Garment

Concept sketch for the Impact Wave biker jacket which hardens on impact in the event of an accident. Dan Plant with Levi Strauss, 2000

Long before smart wearables entered the vocabulary, the Helen Hamlyn Centre for Design was interested in clothing that cares. The idea of designing a garment that provides physical protection or assistance while also being comfortable to wear is an important line of development in supporting the independence of older and disabled people.

In 2000, we collaborated with Levi Strauss on the development of a system of flexible body armour, Impact Wave, which could be integrated directly into garments to protect the human body against impact or abrasions. This was a genuinely inclusive piece of design, as applicable to the impact risks of young motorcycle couriers and skateboarders as to hip protection for older osteoporosis sufferers and frequent fallers.

The system comprised two materials combined in multi-layers which stiffen upon impact but flex with the body when protection is not required, thus combining safety with comfort. Technical tests indicated that this innovation was a significant advance in performance on available body armour solutions at the time, which were either too rigid to

Impact Wave flexible body armour designed by Dan Plant, 2000

wear easily or ineffective on impact. The research made a convincing case for commercial investment, which was not forthcoming.

Two years later, we returned to a subject that has been described as the holy grail of the apparel industry and worked with designers Pearlfisher on a modular clothing collection for young people with disabilities, especially those with circulatory difficulties or who require assistance with dressing. The collection combined a smart aesthetic with smart materials, such as heat-regulating and crease-resistant textiles, to make the garments easy to wear. Strategically placed zips, magnetic buttons and Velcro® fasteners made them easy to put on and take off. LED and reflective strip features were added to improve safety for young people out and about.

Projects such as Pearlfisher's collection showed the potential for clothing – which has such a special relationship to the body – to offer therapeutic and practical support. In the years which followed, wearable technology moved on apace and interest in the subject grew enormously too. So it was perhaps inevitable that when I curated an exhibition called *New Old* – which opened at the Design Museum in London in 2017 prior to an international tour – clothing that cares should again be centre-stage.

Designer Yves Behar of Fuseproject was commissioned to create a project indicating the scale of population ageing – and he presented a 'powered clothing' concept in partnership with a Silicon Valley start-up, Superflex. The Aura Power Suit is described as 'a life-altering intelligent garment' with motors, sensors and artificial intelligence embedded into a responsive system. The suit reacts to the body's natural movement, providing muscle support for the wearer's torso, hips and legs in getting up, sitting down or staying upright.

As with our Impact Wave innovation nearly two decades before, the soft suit flexes with the human body. Hard technology components such as motors, batteries and control boards are designed into hexagonal cells attached to fabric origami fold-ins that enable movement in three dimensions and can be removed to clean the garment. The system is modular and scalable, adapting to the muscular needs and heights of different users. It is an idea whose time has perhaps come at last.

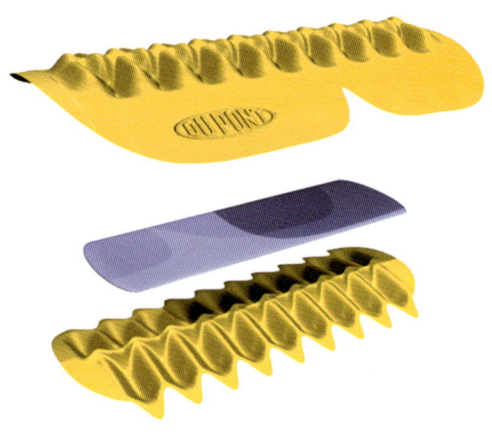

Impact Wave: layered material stiffens on impact

GARMENT

Smart Wearables for young people with disabilities: designed by Pearlfisher, 2002

DESIGNING A WORLD FOR EVERYONE

left
The Aura Power Suit by Yves Behar of Fuseproject: special commission for a Design Museum exhibition, 2017

below
The Aura Power Suit in development in Fuseproject's San Francisco studio

right, *top*
Early prototype on show in the *New Old* exhibition curated by Jeremy Myerson at the Kaohsiung Museum of Fine Arts, Taiwan, 2018

right, bottom
The Aura Power Suit flexes with the human body, providing muscle support for daily movements

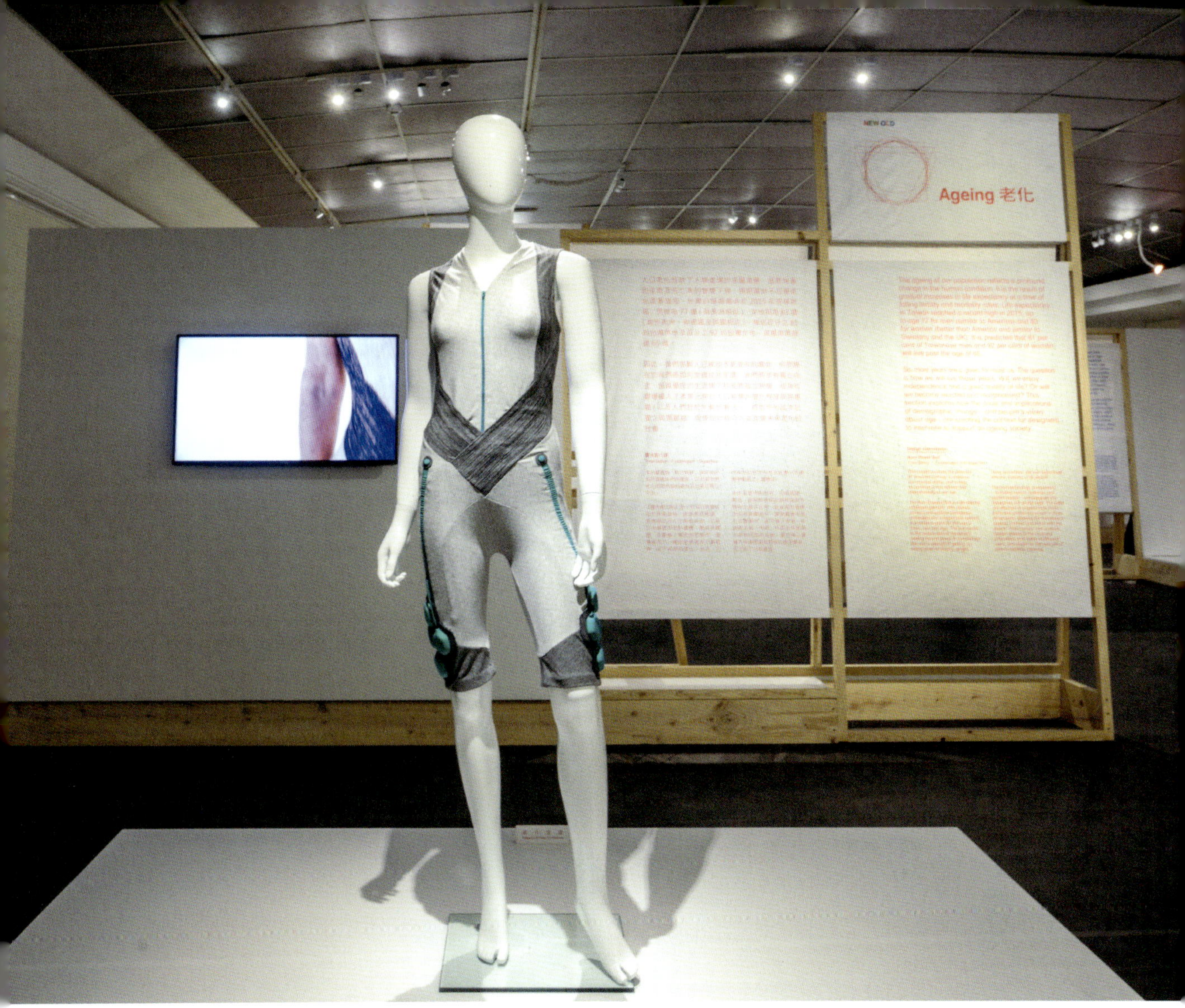

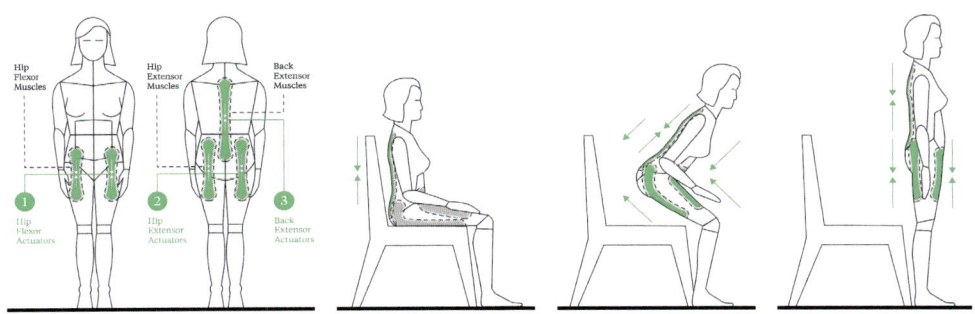

57

Hospital

'First, do no harm' is the Hippocratic oath that every medical student must take. But, despite this laudable principle, one in ten hospital patients in the UK suffers unintended harm as a result of medical error. It's true, hospitals can be bad for your health. To counter this alarming trend, there has been concentrated work over the past 20 years on design for patient safety in the British hospital environment – and the Helen Hamlyn Centre for Design has been at the centre of the action.

Our work began in 2003 with a co-authored report for the Department of Health, 'Design for Patient Safety', which set out a blueprint for a more systematic design approach to healthcare. This was followed by a range of multi-disciplinary research projects in hospitals which explored safety from two different perspectives: first, the performance of clinical staff in reducing medical error; and second, the wellbeing and dignity of hospital patients. On each project, we worked in a collaborative way with hospital clinicians, managers, psychologists, ergonomists, manufacturers, researchers and other experts.

To encourage safer clinical practices in hospital, we worked with academics at Imperial College London to map the conditions in which hospital staff work and study how other sectors, such as the oil exploration, shipping, chemical and mining industries, manage safety processes. Our observations led to a number of innovations on surgical wards, such as the Carecentre, an all-in-one unit for the equipment needed for patient care at the bedside.

This design contains gloves, aprons, sanitising hand gel, cleaning wipes, a medication locker and a clinical waste bin in one unit, and has a sloping flat surface for reading and writing documents. It is located at the end of every bed, with the gloves,

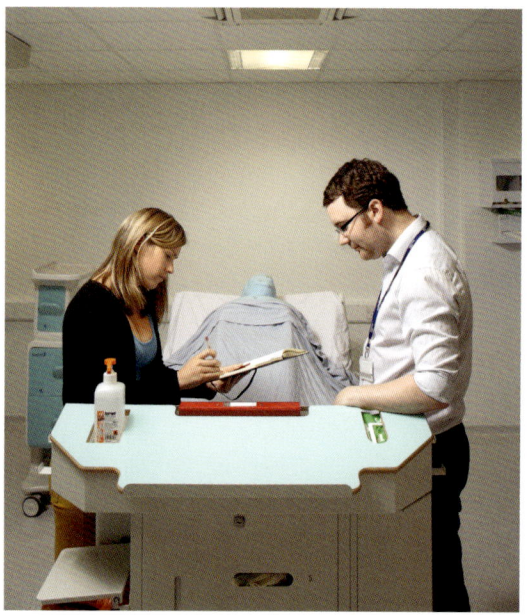

Researchers Grace Davey and Jonathan West position the Carecentre on a simulation ward at St Mary's Hospital in London

apron and gel – so vital to infection control – made much more readily accessible to nurses and doctors. The unit allows staff to focus on providing better patient care in one concentrated area rather than running around looking for disparate pieces of equipment.

In a similar vein, we redesigned the mobile resuscitation trolley – known as the 'crash trolley' – to make it easier for the clinical team on the ward to respond to cardiac emergencies. The crash trolley carries defibrillators, drugs, airway equipment and more to the patient's side. We

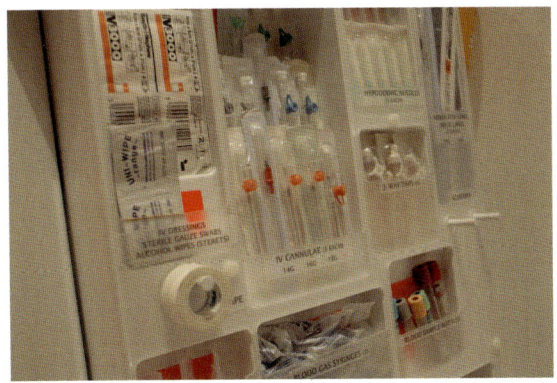

The Resus:station divides into three, making it easier for medical teams to respond to a cardiac arrest

devised a new unit in which the trolley can divide into three separate parts so that each member of the 'crash team' can have their own kit beside them. Staff run around less; stock is tagged with RFID (Radio Frequency Identification) technology; and the entire process is 'logged' using new technology to enable better post-incident evaluation by medical staff.

Both the new crash trolley – the Resus:station – and the Carecentre were commercialised by UK manufacturer Bristol Maid to support safer clinical practice. Other design studies looked at ways to improve the patient experience. We worked with the Design Council and the Department of Health on a series of demonstrator projects to enhance patient dignity and to make hospitals cleaner places so that patients could avoid contracting 'super-bugs'. The work resulted in range of products including: a retractable fabric screen that folds out concertina-style to flexibly divide hospital wards, creating a lightweight barrier between male and female patients; a redesigned cuff for blood pressure measurement with wipe-down polystyrene and magnetic closures to replace Velcro® fastenings, thus making it easier to keep clean; and a hospital gown designed specifically for use by intensive care patients.

Later research into the intensive care experience of critically ill patients, who remain conscious while heavily sedated, revealed opportunities for innovation in the digital realm: we developed an app called Senso as part of a system, trialled in four hospitals, to create personalised sensory experiences for each individual to relieve stress and anxiety through soothing imagery, sounds and aromas.

Our focus on hospital safety extended to the waiting areas of Accident & Emergency departments, where harmful incidents of patient violence and assault consistently disrupt medical treatments. Our researchers were part of a large team that traced the causes of aggression, profiled typical perpetrators and redesigned the arrival and waiting experience with new signs, furniture, lighting and online information to remove frustrations and create a more understandable and empathic system. A package of improvements was tested in three hospitals.

The Carecentre sits at the foot of the hospital bed, providing an all-in-one unit for patient care

HOSPITAL

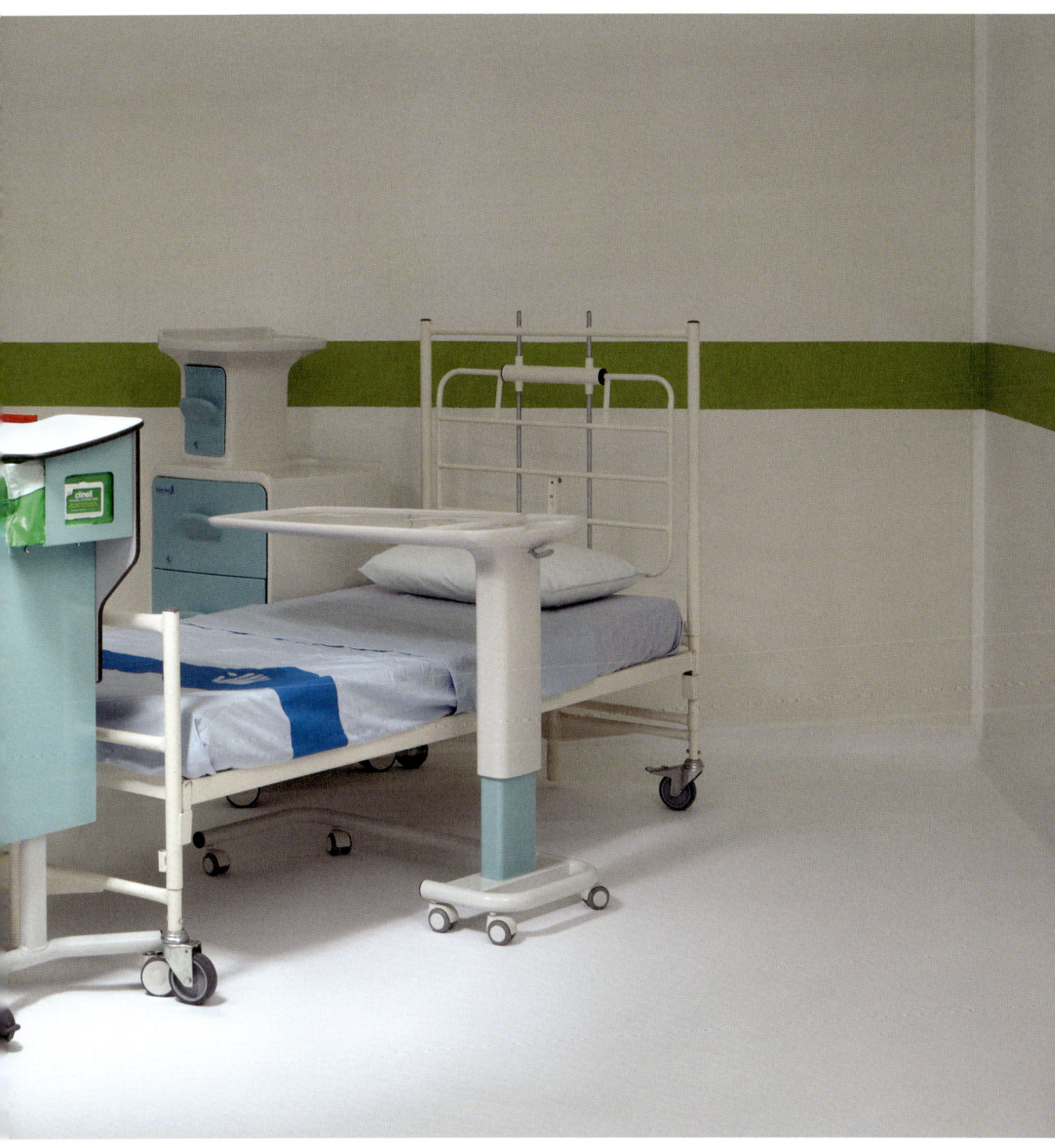

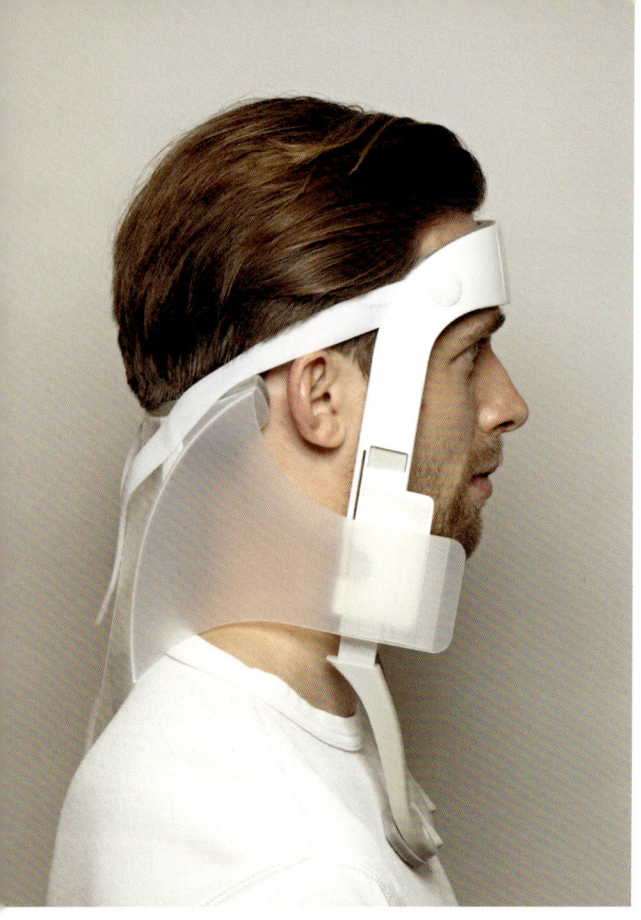

We also looked at improving standard pieces of medical equipment such as the neck brace, which is used to stabilise the patient's head and neck after a suspected spinal injury but which has several drawbacks. An extensive programme of user research resulted in the design of a new, easier-to-use neck brace better able to fit a variety of body sizes, increase immobilisation, enhance comfort and improve clinical access when doctors need to perform tests. A collaboration with a manufacturer, DePuy Johnson & Johnson, led to a redesign of surgical tools to make them safer and easier to use.

left
Neck brace redesigned for ease of clinical use, 2013

below
Pulse oximeter redesigned for easier cleaning: Design Bugs Out project, 2009

bottom
Cannula time tracker gives nurses advance warning and avoids the risk of infection: Design Bugs Out project, 2009

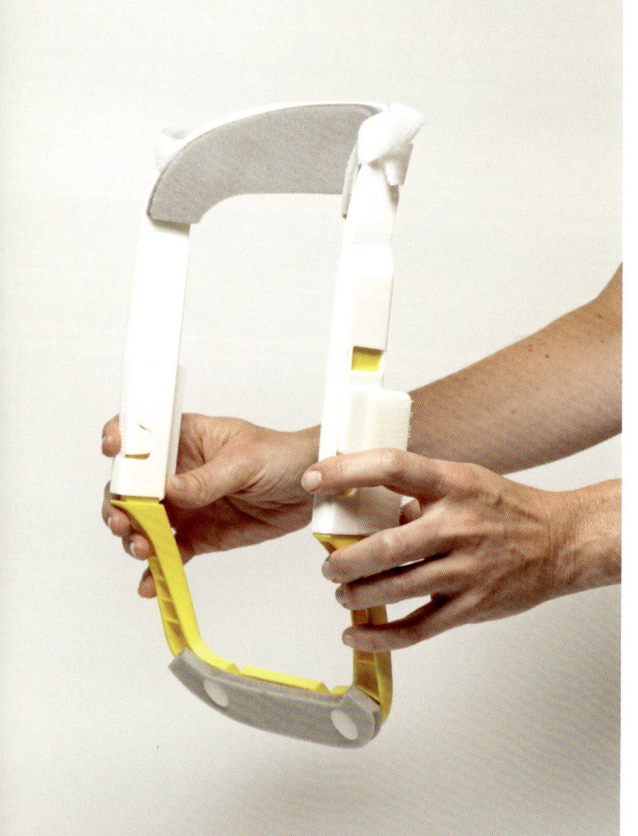

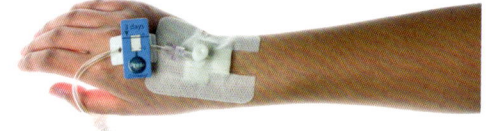

Senso system combines physical and digital elements to improve the experience of intensive care patients, 2016

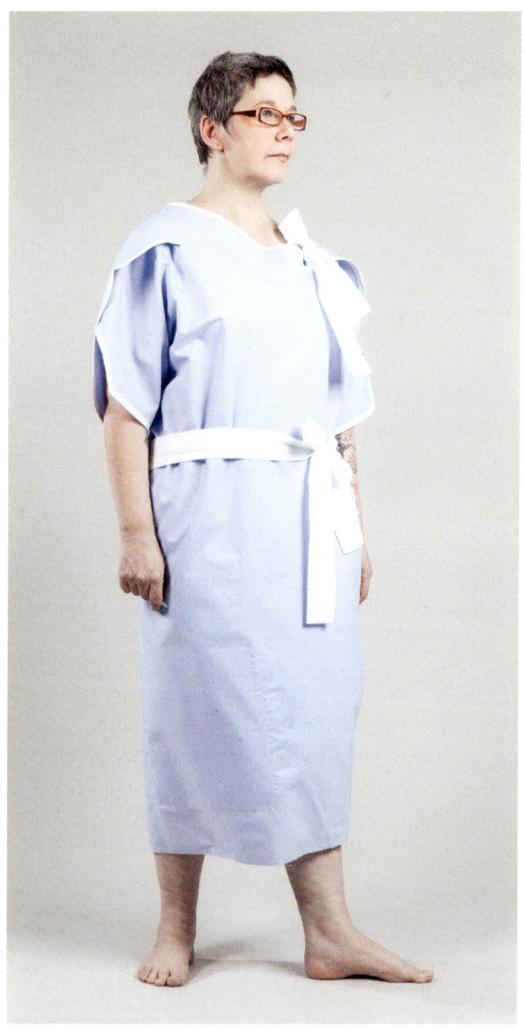

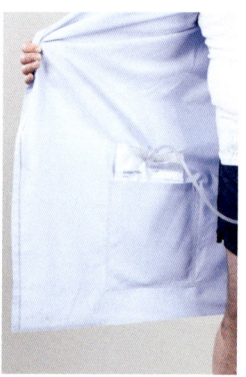 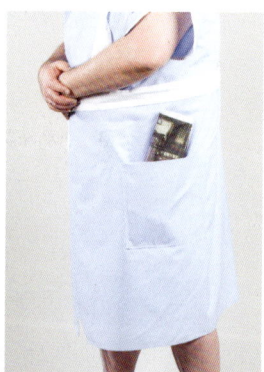

left and below
Hospital gowns designed for use by intensive care patients: Design for Patient Dignity project, 2010

left, bottom
Nurses try on a blood pressure cuff designed for easier cleaning: Design Bugs Out project, 2009

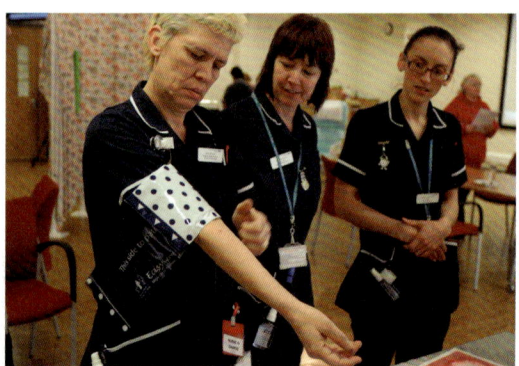

Our work in hospitals not only led to the design of new equipment and services but generated new methods for working in multi-disciplinary teams. On typical healthcare projects, clinicians, psychologists, designers and manufacturers tend to work in isolation on their own phases of development, 'passing the baton' to each other as in a relay race. Every time the 'baton' is passed on, there is the potential to lose vital information which dilutes the original intended clinical purpose. We evolved a different methodology, more akin to the rowing team. All the different players are 'in the same boat' and actively involved in every stage of development. There is the opportunity for the whole team to learn from other disciplines. As a result, the designs that emerge are more suited to the clinical environment and contribute more effectively to reducing harm.

Surgical tool redesigned for patient safety, replacing the metal instrument with a plastic device. Project with DePuy Johnson & Johnson, 2007

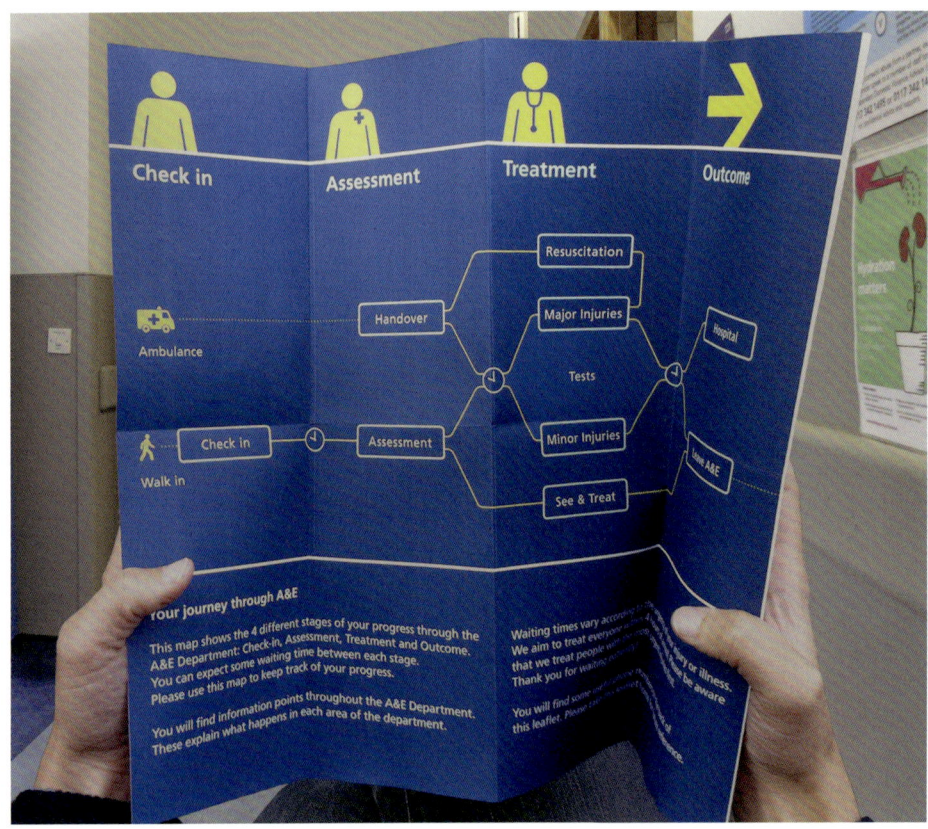

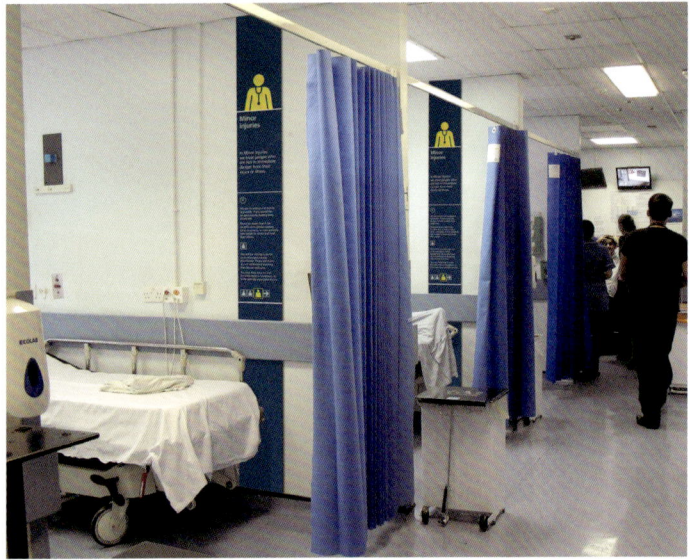

Information system to address violence and aggression in hospital Accident & Emergency departments, 2011

HOSPITAL

top
A mixed-sex hospital ward before the deployment of a flexible fabric screen to divide the space, Design for Patient Dignity project, 2010

middle
The screen folds out concertina style to provide a barrier that is more rigid than a curtain, but just as easy for a nursing team to pull across

bottom
Diagram explaining the technical properties of the design. A double layer of tensioned fabric is stretched across an aluminium stud framework

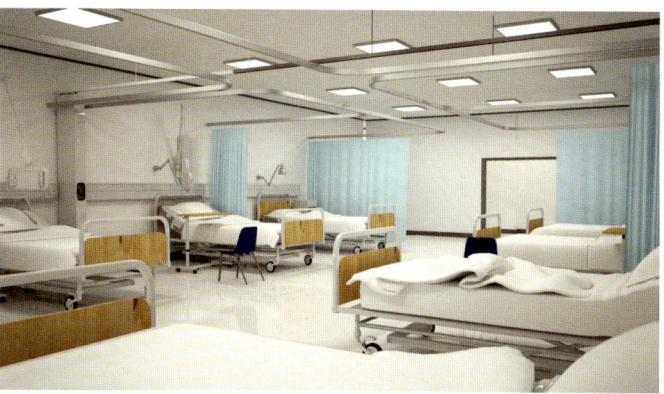

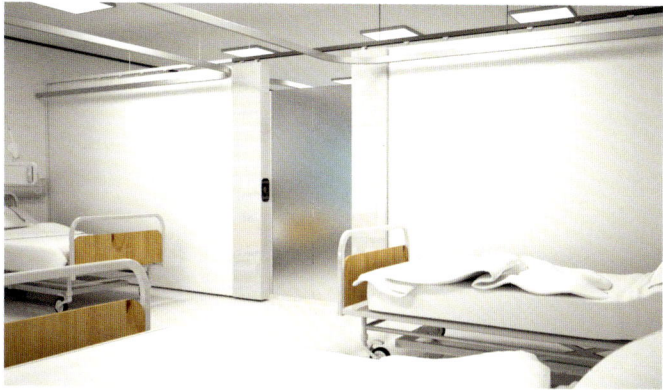

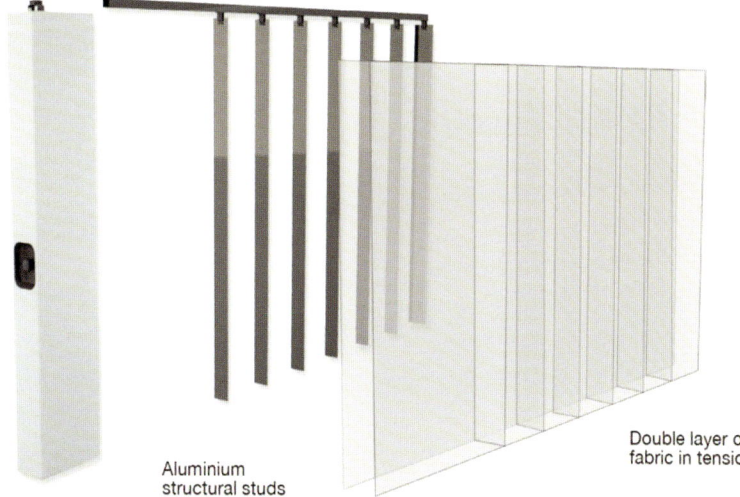

Kitchen

Cooking is an essential and enjoyable activity of daily living, but not everyone can participate equally. Take people with osteoarthritis, for example; this is an age-related condition which affects the joints, with more women than men experiencing the condition. The loss of dexterity and associated pain in the hands can make cooking a struggle. We worked with a leading arthritis charity to explore how kitchen equipment and processes could be redesigned to make it easier for people with osteoarthritis to prepare meals.

Our researchers worked alongside occupational therapists in London to engage with people across a range of ethnic and cultural backgrounds with varying degrees of arthritis. What we discovered was that the best form of therapeutic intervention was to keep people exercising their hands by challenging their dexterity. To do this, we created a 'hand healthy' recipe book of traditional meals that require persistent hand movements such as kneading dough, translating the everyday activity of cooking into a gentle and accessible form of exercise.

Our research team also developed a new device called the Kitchen Anchor which assists with grip when peeling, grating or chopping. This innovation fixes a metal utensil such as a grater or peeler to a chopping board with a non-slip mat, leaving the user with both hands free to apply more pressure to the task.

Kitchen Anchor, designed by Simon Kinneir, assists people with osteoarthritis to prepare food, 2014

On a project with Factory Design as part of the DBA Inclusive Design Challenge, people with severe arthritis told us that they all loved cooking but their moment of truth in the kitchen came once the dish was ready and had to be lifted from the heat source. It was then that the weight and design of the saucepan increased the pain of their condition and led to accidents. We also talked to visually impaired cooks with a different set of issues relating more to safety and hygiene. Factory Design's challenge was to create a saucepan that would address all these needs.

Saucepan designed to support cooking by people with arthritis: Factory Design, 2004

Handle detail on the Factory Design saucepan

The design team came up with a new form for the saucepan based on a universal pan size to accommodate different cooking methods – it has a traditional circular shape but incorporates conical sides for easy pouring and a large radius to facilitate cleaning. The body is made of aluminium for lightness of weight, with a non-stick interior for easier cleaning and a copper bottom for better heat distribution. It also has an integrated aluminium colander for drainage and a two-part lid in transparent polycarbonate and aluminium, with a hooped handle that is easy to lift.

A major feature of the new design is the ergonomic, long, two-part handle which radically changes the way in which the user holds the pan. With a fuller cross-section to assist gripping, it shifts the weight of the pan to the arm from a single point at the wrist, ensuring greater balance and safety and less pain. The final prototype was exhibited widely prior to manufacture.

Our research into kitchens not only looked at widening access to cooking in the UK – we also redesigned the traditional Japanese kitchen stove, the *konro*, in a project with Osaka Gas. The *konro* is a familiar feature of most Japanese kitchens – a gas cooker typically comprising three hobs and a fish grill, and unchanged for decades. Mindful of a rapidly ageing population in Japan, Osaka Gas wanted to take a more inclusive approach in which weight, positioning and overall design would seek to reduce the physical effort needed to operate the appliance. The new design incorporated a number of features to make the *konro* safer and easier to use. Naturally, the all-important fish grill was the first component to be fully prototyped in a country where, as one of our Japanese partners wryly pointed out, 'if you throw a stone, it will hit a senior.'

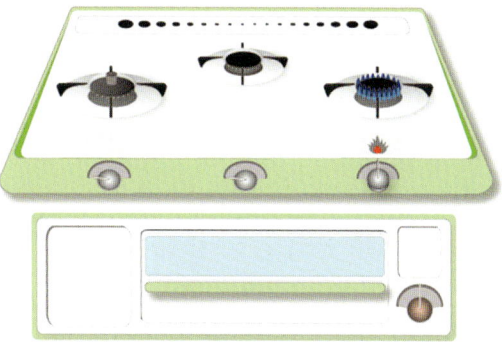

Redesign of a traditional Japanese cooker for Osaka Gas by Chris McGinley, 2004

Light

Illuminated goal posts designed to light a neglected playground on the Boundary Estate in London, 2012

Light is central to all our visual experience and over the past 30 years our researchers have looked at light and lighting from a variety of angles. Projects have ranged from office lighting that changes with the circadian rhythm of the working day to lighting for the home that supports older people with sight loss or seasonal affective disorder. We have even investigated the nature of light itself in a project exploring the negative effects of over-illumination and glare on people's wellbeing.

But perhaps our most important contribution has been in the realm of working with urban communities to light inner-city neighbourhoods in a more inclusive way. Urban lighting is unevenly distributed. While well-heeled business districts and tourist areas are often brightly lit at night, more residential pockets of the inner-city are under-lit, leaving economically deprived local communities literally in the dark, limiting trade and use of public space, and undermining social cohesion.

Our interest in this issue began in 2002 with a study of public lighting design in London; this led to a project to use light to regenerate London's Kentish Town Road, transforming a tough inner-city district into a vibrant thoroughfare. The proposals were installed by the London Borough of Camden. We then worked in another London borough, Tower Hamlets, in 2004 on a social housing project on the St Peter's Estate in Bethnal Green to demonstrate how lighting and landscaping could improve under-utilised communal spaces. Both projects involved extensive consultation and workshops with local residents.

We subsequently took this collaborative approach to lighting the inner city into a third, ethnically mixed urban neighbourhood, the Boundary Estate in Shoreditch, London, in 2011. Workshops were held with three different groups – local older people, Bengali men and a group of young Bengali-British women – to map use of the housing estate after dark as part of an in-depth engagement with residents. Our research revealed that lack of place-sensitive lighting was a barrier to certain groups using their own neighbourhood. Security floodlighting used in conjunction with CCTV was resented.

An alternative lighting strategy was therefore proposed based on the concept of a 'night-time neighbourhood network'. Within a dark local

Drawing shows the insertion of an LED strip into a standard scaffolding tube

Prototype LED light tube creates a low-cost, low-energy system to light the estate

area, more brightly lit 'nodes' could be designed to encourage activity at existing or newly built community facilities. Bus stops, benches, shopfronts, trees and playgrounds could become joints in a 'light skeleton', creating safe, inclusive areas for evening activities. This concept was endorsed by local residents, but how could this light skeleton be realised technically?

At this point, a member of our research team, designer Tom Jarvis, had a Eureka moment on the project. Cycling around the

Lighting concept for St Peter's housing estate in Bethnal Green, London, by Matthew Dearlove, 2004

Boundary Estate one day, he noticed an abundance of scaffolding poles and clamps which are widely used by local authorities to form gates, fences, barriers, handrails, bike racks and play equipment in the public realm. He immediately recognised their potential to create a versatile new lighting system for the estate by adapting a standard scaffolding tube to house an LED strip.

Through design development and on-site testing, a complete range of tubular LED components was created that enables existing public objects such as benches or bike racks to become luminaires in themselves. The network-of-light concept was realised by repurposing existing infrastructure – nothing new was added to the environment. A permanent installation of illuminated goalposts was built on a neglected playground on the Boundary Estate to test the concept, supported by Tower Hamlets officials and the police who were concerned about crime after dark.

The project led directly to the setting up of a new lighting company to make and market the innovation. It also marked a significant first step in demonstrating an alternative approach to providing better lighting for local urban communities, who are so often overlooked in terms of investment in the infrastructure of the city.

Lighting for the regeneration of Kentish Town Road by Harry Dobbs, based on a 2002 research study

Medication

When it comes to labelling on medicines, graphic design can be a matter of life or death. More medication is now being prescribed in the UK than ever before: the number of prescriptions dispensed by community pharmacies has passed one billion for the first time. But poor information design on medicine packs can mean that patients either receive the wrong drug from the pharmacy or take the wrong dose, with the result that they become hospitalised.

We worked closely with the NHS National Patient Safety Agency (NPSA) to create better information design guidelines for medication. Our research followed the 'journey of the pack' from manufacturer to hospitals, pharmacies and patients. We concentrated on the blister pack as this was found to be the most widely used type of packaging for prescription-only medicines. Special attention was given to colour, type size and style, and hierarchies of information. The project resulted

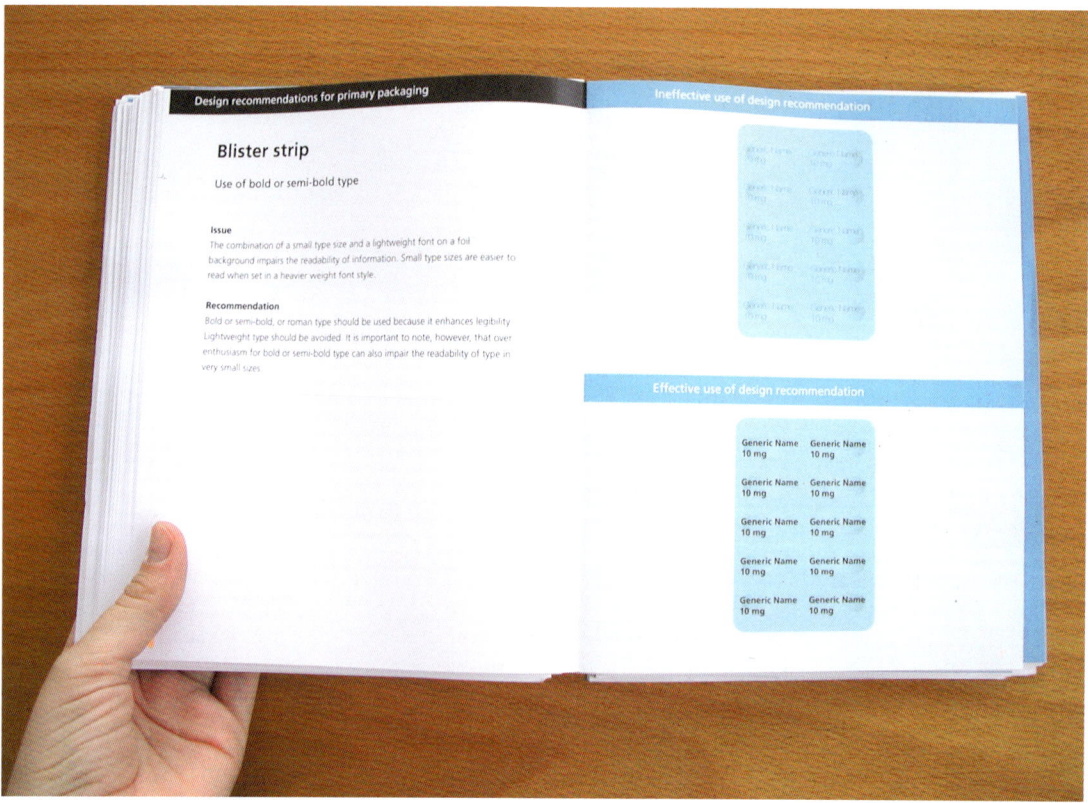

A sample spread giving graphic design guidelines for blister packs, National Patient Safety Agency, 2005

MEDICATION

Researcher Thea Swayne (right) discusses the use of medication with a research participant

in the publication of a set of consistent graphic design principles – an important contribution to reducing medication errors attributed to confusing and unwieldy information design.

We subsequently worked with the NPSA to develop graphic design principles for the packaging of injectable medicines and single-use medical devices. But our work in medication was not confined to public sector graphics. We also collaborated with a manufacturer, GlaxoSmithKline, to incorporate three-dimensional compliance aids into packaging. This project focused on making it easier for older people, who take three times as many drugs as the general population, to access the right dose of the right drug at the right time.

To do this, our research team created a range of solutions including an easy-access pack with a matchbox-style opening mechanism, a pack with a special box detachable from the main pack to support discreet use of medication while on the move, and a reminder pack with a collection of prompts such as stickers and cards that could be removed from the pack and placed around the home as personal prompts to take the prescribed medication.

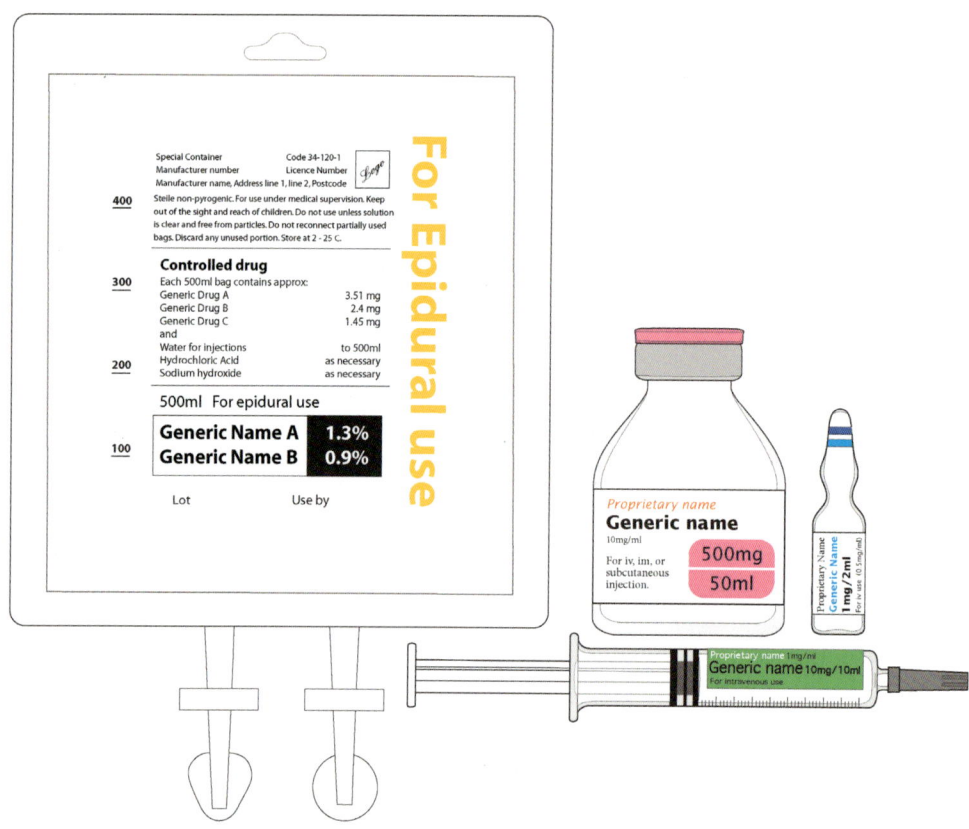

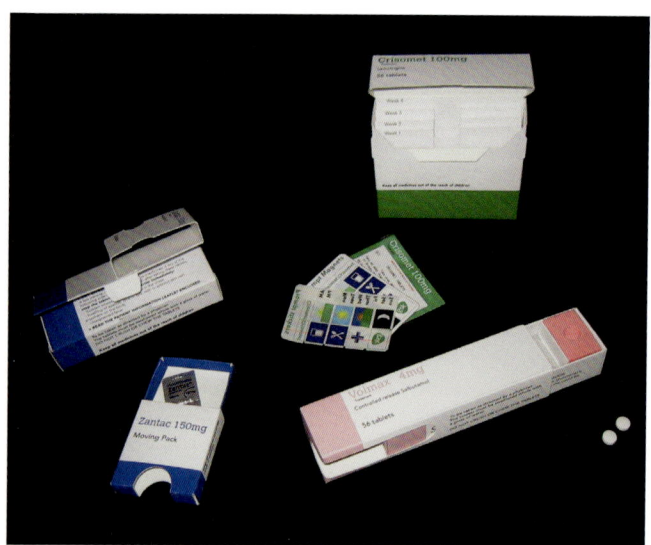

above

Graphic design guidance for injectable medicines to reduce medical error, 2007

left

Packaging concepts for GlaxoSmithKline to aid compliance in taking medication, 2004

Mobile Phone

The mobile phone was the size of a large brick in the earliest days of the Helen Hamlyn Centre for Design and not yet on the radar of inclusive design. But very quickly, mobile phone technology began to shrink in physical size while expanding its influence across every sphere of daily living, promising many benefits for older and disabled people. Our work in this area has largely concentrated on making the mobile phone more accessible for older age groups.

In 2003, we worked with designers Seymour Powell on 'Ello, a winning entry to the DBA Inclusive Design Challenge. This stripped the mobile phone down to its essentials minus the screen for more intuitive use: the design team produced a compact folding device with easy-to-open 'book edges' for one-handed use and a keypad that rises when opened to give increased tactile feedback. Four years later, we worked with BT on a smart new device called the Two-Tone Phone which combined a normal cordless house phone on one side of the unit with an internet-enabled one on the other.

While innovative, both of these solutions were 'special phones' for a special needs group. Meanwhile, our research was beginning to tell us something different. Older people didn't want a special age-friendly phone that could be seen as stigmatising. Instead, they wanted mainstream mobile phone technology the same as everyone else that was easier and simpler to set up.

In 2009, we were asked by Samsung to investigate this issue. We discovered that the joy of owning a new mobile phone can be quickly lost as soon as you take the device out of the box, try to learn to use it and struggle with the manual. Older people can have a particularly frustrating experience as they apply analogue ways of learning to the digital experience, looking in the

'Ello mobile phone for older people: designed by Seymour Powell, 2004

box for help that simply is not there. Creative workshops with user groups in the UK, Italy and Norway led to the development of a new type of instruction manual that turns the throwaway manual into a hardcover book designed to be kept on a shelf and referred to throughout the life of the phone.

Many older people ask friends or family to talk them through the phone set-up, so the pages of the book mimic this process using a conversational tone that is devoid of technological jargon. Turning the pages reveals step-by-step instructions, with graphical and text-based

Innovative storybook concept for Samsung to provide instructions to set up a mobile phone: Clara Gaggero Westaway and Adrian Westaway, 2009

instructions pointing to the actual device and accessories, which are encased within the pages of the book, minimising chances for error. The book then takes the user through other phone functions using the same process.

This concept was exhibited at the Museum of Modern Art, New York, and elements were earmarked for development by Samsung. It exemplified a simple approach to humanising digital technology for marginalised groups – in this case, using an analogue storybook interface – that avoided the trap of designing a special phone. It was a strategy we would explore on other mobile phone projects. With Nokia, we created a concept for older people called Chalk that transferred data from the standard phone to a large electronic chalkboard – a familiar object – for increased readability of messages. With Blackberry, we worked with visually impaired users to develop a series of visual, audio and tactile sliders to enable them to customise the smartphone to their precise needs.

Another Blackberry project looked at how to respond to the communication needs of the multi-generational family, recognising that teenagers want a different level of digital functionality from their grandparents. This research, part of a series, fed into the Blackberry for Life campaign that repositioned the brand from a business tool to a much broader lifestyle device playing an intimate role in all our daily activities.

By now, we were witnessing the rise of the Quantified Self (QS) movement, in which young 'everyday athletes' used digital technology to maintain their fitness by measuring sleep patterns, body fat, heart rate, steps taken, calories eaten and so on. But in a project with Panasonic, we discovered that older people were far less interested in wearing devices and generating lots of empirical data on their performance. Instead they wanted the technology to support their sense of self by delivering personal insights into their own health and wellbeing – so we redefined the Quantified Self as the Qualified Self (QLS) movement and produced some concept designs to show how it might work.

In less than a decade, our focus as a research centre on mobile phone use extended from the physical artefact to systems and software. Today, whatever the subject, there is hardly a research project that doesn't have a dimension related to smartphone apps.

Two-Tone Phone for BT designed by Matthew Harrison and Cian Plumbe, 2007

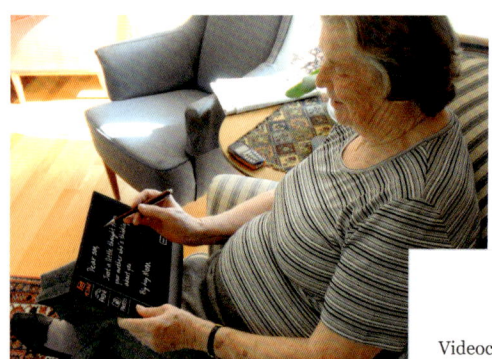

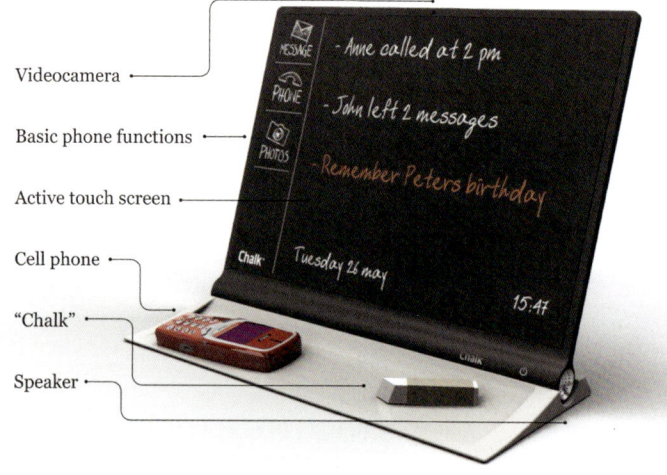

Chalk concept for Nokia devised by a Norwegian design team, Oslo, 2008

Visual, audio and tactile sliders enable visually impaired users to customise their Blackberry: Maja Kecman and Yusuf Muhammad, 2009

Office

There's an old joke about nobody on their deathbed ever wishing they'd spent more time in the office and it rarely fails to raise a smile. But beyond this familiar gag lies a darker truth about the place where we spend so much of our lives – the experience of working regularly in an office is not associated with being an especially pleasant or uplifting one. Workplace design has tended to prioritise management efficiency over the wellbeing of workers. Office buildings have generally been constructed from a technical perspective, using engineering, technology and mathematics to determine optimum conditions for productivity.

The trouble with this approach is that the human beings who work in offices aren't nearly as rational as the data on which their workplaces are constructed – they often behave in ways that defy the logic of technical systems. Today, office workers increasingly crave flexibility, community and sensory experiences. There's a backlash against time-and-motion workplaces that treat people like cogs in a machine. The Helen Hamlyn Centre for Design has worked extensively with the workplace industry for over 20 years to research a new behavioural design agenda for a more human-centric office based around such issues as wellbeing, experience and sensation.

As part of this work, we anticipated one of the most significant current trends in office design. This is the rise of biophilic design – bringing nature into the workplace, whether in the form of plants and trees, natural materials, nature imagery, access to outdoor workspace or natural ventilation and sunlight. Biophilic design is today scientifically proven to reduce stress, but long before it was validated in the commercial workplace, we were experimenting with its effects.

In 2008, we created a biophilic design intervention as part of an international study called Welcoming Workplace, which looked at ways to improve the wellbeing and motivation

'Rain curtain' of falling water fronts a green contemplation space in the London office of a pharmaceutical company: Welcoming Workplace project, 2008

of older office workers. This comprised a 'rain curtain' of falling water, an office garden, adjustable furniture for rest and recuperation, and a soundscape of birdsong. It was a setting designed as an oasis for contemplation, which was identified as the missing link in workplace design.

Offices at the time provided spaces for concentration (usually rows of open-plan desks) and collaboration (glass-box meeting rooms). But there was little space for escape and reflection. Our contemplation zone was prototyped and tested in organisations in the UK, Japan and Australia. We quickly learnt that not only older workers appreciated this innovation – all ages felt burnt out and in need of a soothing break during the working day. Our inclusive design framework, combining concentration, collaboration and contemplation spaces, was subsequently adopted by several office developers and occupiers, including the developer of The Shard at London Bridge – the tallest building in the UK – designed by Italian architect Renzo Piano.

If bringing the outdoors in was one office design strategy we helped to pioneer, then making the interior more flexible and expressive was another. Many offices were criticised for their monotony and rigidity – and for their lack of psychological stimulus – even when well-engineered. To create more visual and operational variety, some companies created spectacular, highly customised, one-off workplaces, but these proved to be expensive and difficult to build. So, we looked at ways to create expressive and engaging office interiors more simply and at lower cost. We studied the history and background of theatre design to define a vocabulary of inexpensive but highly effective stage elements to create mood and atmosphere in the workplace.

A modular 'kit-of-parts' approach was developed around the application of light, shadow, projection, screens, levels, colour and vista. Our research team demonstrated its practical potential by working with two manufacturers to design a single manifestation of the approach: an illuminated screen system, capable of suspension from the ceiling, to support private concentration and informal collaboration in the open-plan office. This used the same principles as a theatre set being 'flown in' from above. We tested different screen systems with 60 office workers, evaluating such variables as translucency (low to high), colour (calm to vivid), illumination (soft to intense) and arrangement (open to closed) in order to better understand people's sensory preferences in the workplace.

Through studies such as these, we recognised how different types of environment – from theatres to libraries – held important lessons for creating a more psychologically enriched office space. We looked in particular at the dynamism and spontaneity of temporary events in cities such as markets, festivals and pop-ups, distilling key elements to inform a new approach. We came to see the workplace as a combination of process and experience – the office was no longer just about the work people did, but also how they felt about it.

In a parallel project, we continued the urban theme and adopted an architectural framework derived from Parc de la Villette in Paris to explore how workspace could be redesigned to be more socially dynamic for its inhabitants. Using a combination of programmable surfaces, circulation routes, large objects and points of interaction to adjust the workspace in response to behavioural requirements, this study generated an online toolkit for a global furniture company to plan more people-centred office environments.

In the global coronavirus pandemic of 2020, the clock stopped and the office was suddenly out of reach for millions of employees around the world who were told to 'shelter-in-place'. Remote working accelerated amid concerns over office safety and hygiene. Today, a new landscape of work is emerging in which the office is taking on a new purpose as a carefully planned destination for collaboration and social interaction, rather than for routine daily work. It is this new context that gives our research around behaviour, experience and wellbeing an enhanced relevance.

left

A 'rain curtain' brings a natural element into the artificial office environment

below

Concept sketch by Catherine Greene for the rain curtain and a mobile office garden for employees to tend

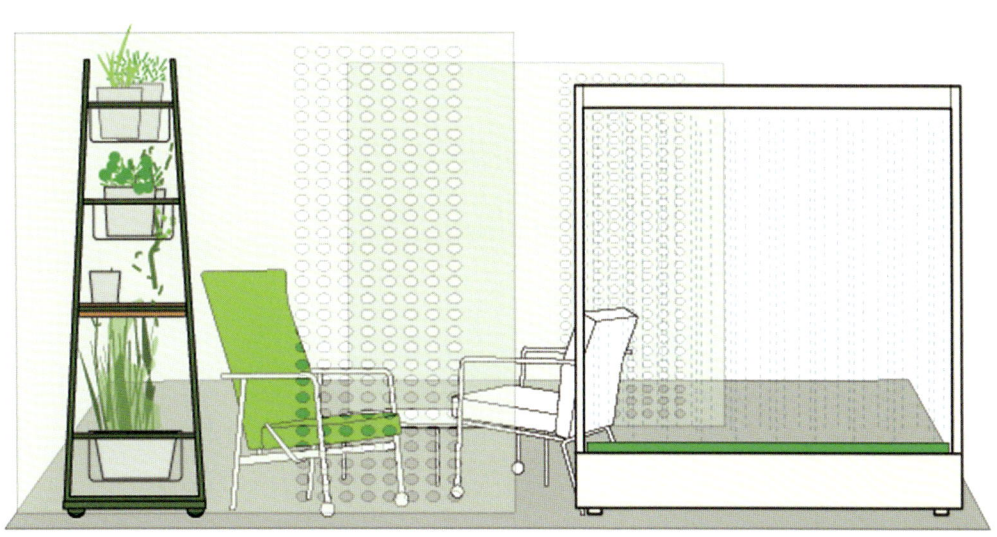

DESIGNING A WORLD FOR EVERYONE

below
Designer Tom Jarvis (left) observes as office workers test his prototype enclosure based on theatre design techniques: Haworth showroom, London, 2013

right, *top*
Lightweight hanging banners and framing devices drawn from stage design create a new-look office environment: concept by architectural researcher Imogen Privett, 2012

right, *bottom*
Concept by Imogen Privett for lightweight coloured screens showing how office space can be enlivened

85

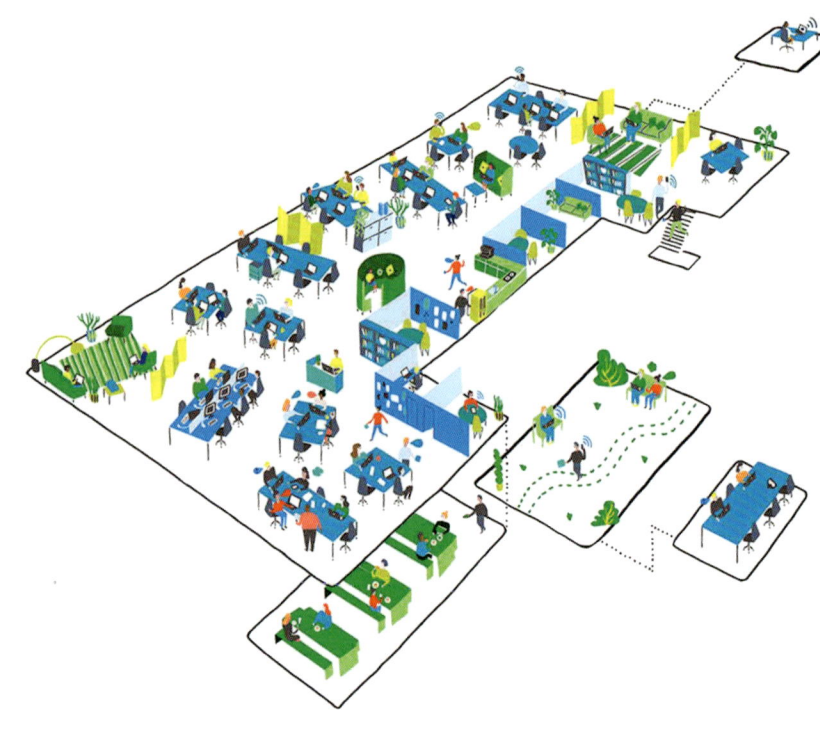

right

Office floorplate using architectural planning principles to adapt a workspace to human needs: Workscapes project, 2014

below right

The same floorplate in the Workscapes project reduced to essentials of programmable surfaces, circulation routes, large objects and points of interaction

bottom

Workscapes research translated into an online office planning tool for Herman Miller

Park

Model showing the concept for Inspiration Park, based on research with disabled people. Design by Imagination, 2001

One of London's greatest assets is the large number of urban parks and garden squares that form a welcome part of the cityscape. But these open spaces are not welcoming to everyone. People with visual impairments can find parks difficult to navigate, as they lack the essential auditory cues that the built environment typically provides. Wheelchair users can get bogged down in mud and sodden earth. Individuals with sensory and cognitive differences can feel exposed. So, we researched how an urban park could be designed that was not only non-threatening to a diverse range of users, but also a place of fun, relaxation and inspiration.

In 2001, we worked with a design team at Imagination and a selected group of young people with different disabilities to explore visual concepts for an inclusive, all-weather urban park landscaped with a range of multi-sensory features. The footprint of Russell Square, then undergoing

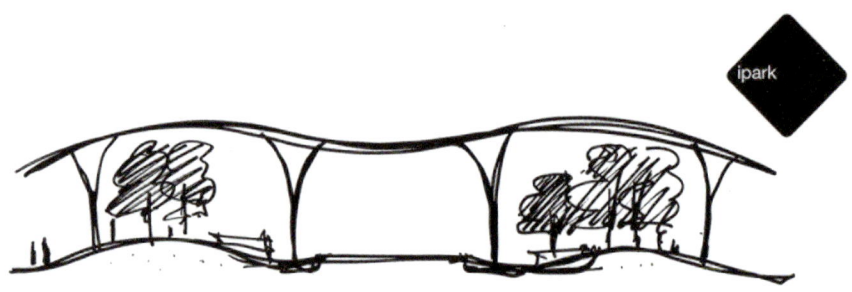

Concept sketch for an enclosed park

refurbishment, was chosen for the project. The environment was conceived as a circular, covered space where four approach paths meet, divided into separate areas for water, art, nature and play.

This space was designed as the centrepiece – a meeting place for all visitors where a table-top pond, overflowing with constant running water, could provide a relaxing soundscape. Sensory features included a vertical water wall, over-sized bamboo wind chimes, tactile sculptures, texture walls lined with different types of rock, pressure-activated sound tiles to play music and scented wall climbers. On rainy days, the water would funnel down through a circular opening in the transparent roof. The pathways were constructed in a safe, tough compound rubber, providing a consistent surface that would be comfortable to walk on and ideal for pushchairs, wheelchairs and long cane users.

Inspiration Park, as the project was named, was studied closely by local authorities in London. It demonstrated that inclusive public space was about much more than just barrier-free access – it was

also about inspiration and delight. There was even a plan to offset the cost of building and maintaining such a facility by incorporating a large text scroller in the park to display news and information, which could be sponsored. Inspiration Park won the 2001 DBA Inclusive Design Challenge.

Inspiration Park by Imagination, 2001: concept for a London square features interactive sound tiles that play music

Inspiration Park details focus on water, art, nature and play

Power Tool

One of the ironies of growing older is having the time to carry out basic home improvement tasks in retirement only to discover that the do-it-yourself tools available to buy are too heavy and difficult to use. In 2000, we were approached by Europe's largest home improvement retailer, B&Q, with market data showing a decline in sales of their DIY products such as drills, screwdrivers and sanders among the over-60s, despite research from the Henley Centre for Forecasting indicating a strong desire among older people to carry out essential maintenance in their homes. How could we explain this?

Our answer was to audit B&Q's own-brand power tools with a group of older customers in a series of user workshops. The company's senior executives could see for themselves that their products were not designed for those with failing eyesight or reduced grip. Some tools were so heavy that they could barely be lifted off the table; others were criticised for being too complex. The project also studied how older carpenters managed to cope professionally with reduced strength. Two new product concepts were then developed: a compact, pebble-shaped cordless screwdriver called Gofer; and a palm-sized sander called Sandbug with an innovative hand strap.

Cordless screwdrivers are among the most popular power tools. However, their long, unwieldy shape can make them difficult to grip and activate. A redesign made the shape easier to fit into the palm of the hand, while its foreshortened design allowed

Best-selling, assistive B&Q power tools by Matthew White, packaged for mainstream appeal, 2002

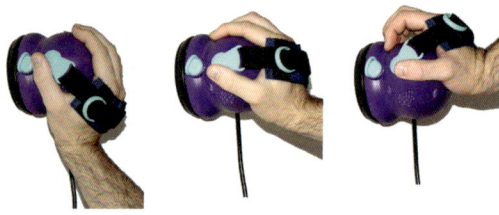

Use of a palm-sized sander supported by a hand strap

it to be used in corners that were inaccessible to screwdrivers of conventional length. The tool was also designed so that it automatically activates as soon as the screw bit locks into the screw head.

Conventional palm-sized sanders are generally uncomfortable to hold, as the user is expected to press and hold a sander against a surface to re-create a sanding motion while it vibrates. The tool can tend to slip sideways due to this motion, leaving the user to grip, hold and steer simultaneously. Our sander was redesigned to 'cup' the hand, while a hand strap eliminated the need to grip it firmly.

Ethnographic study of older carpenters informed the project

Members of the University of the Third Age test B&Q's existing range of power tools

Both the screwdriver and the sander were prototyped, evaluated and brought to the market by B&Q by Christmas 2002. The branding and packaging for these new power tools was modern and mainstream, with no hint that they might be assistive devices. Our Research Associate on the project, Matthew White, joined the company as a design consultant and began a long-term relationship with B&Q to extend the range.

Not only did the new power tools enjoy substantial commercial success in the UK but they were also best-sellers in China where B&Q had built a major presence. Today, the study remains one of the most important in the history of the Helen Hamlyn Centre for Design as it was the first major demonstration of the commercial appeal of inclusive design.

Public Toilet

We all know how difficult it can be to find a toilet when away from the home. For some, such as older people, those with reduced continence due to a medical condition, or people with young children, this can be much more than an inconvenience. In the UK, many public toilets are unhygienic, inaccessible or closed, which compounds the problem. How could we find a way to make public toilets in Britain more available and accessible to the people who need them most?

Our research focused on the needs of two groups: members of the public and providers of publicly accessible toilets. Nearly 100 people were interviewed about their experiences of finding and using public toilets, from parents of new-borns to people aged over 90. Four generic user profiles were created from this research to communicate people's needs. Twenty providers of toilet facilities, from local authorities to shopping centres and train stations, participated in the study, which also looked at misuse and crime prevention in relation to toilet provision.

The project produced two major outputs: a publication entitled 'Inclusive Design Guide to Publicly Accessible Toilets', containing case studies and outlining location-specific problems and potential solutions; and a citizen-driven website named the Great British Public Toilet Map (www.toiletmap.org.uk) that uses open data provided by local councils to give information about public toilets in the UK.

While the design guide was useful to professionals working in the field, the Great British Public Toilet Map proved to be a winning idea with the public. It was conceived in response to information about publicly accessible toilets being incomplete, out of date and fragmented across hundreds of websites. A well-received pilot for the London area was followed by an expansion of the Great British Public Toilet Map across the whole of the UK. Today it lists more than 13,500 facilities from more than 400 local authorities on one site, and also includes data on privately provided toilets that the public may use, such as those in railway stations. There have been more than half a million visitors to the site since it was launched.

The project demonstrates how valuable local open data can be in improving public service provision, particularly in combination with other data sources. It has received extensive national media coverage and exerted an influence on policy – in 2017, a new public health act in Wales required Welsh councils to publish their toilet strategies as a statutory duty. In 2018, seven years after the research first began as a study of incontinence, lead researchers Jo-Anne Bichard and Gail Ramster set up a spin-out company to run the Great British Public Toilet Map. Its name – you guessed it: Public Convenience Ltd.

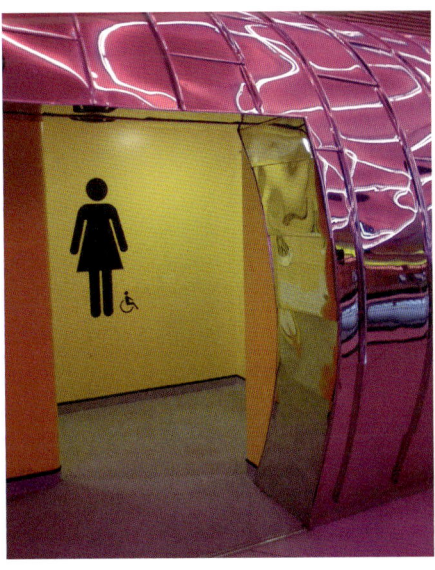

Entrance to the women's facilities at The Public art centre in West Bromwich. The image was chosen for the cover of the inclusive design guide

left

The Great British Public Toilet Map uses open data from local authorities to create a valuable online resource

below

Information about publicly available facilities can be accessed via a smartphone when out and about

right

Researcher Gail Ramster studies public toilet provision for men in Hyde Park, London

River

'Ready for the Foyle' is a familiar saying among residents of Derry-Londonderry in Northern Ireland, a city with a long history of sectarian tension and violence. Whether said in jest or with deadly seriousness, the saying refers to a bleak, six-mile stretch of the River Foyle which is a well-known suicide black spot. In 2016, the Helen Hamlyn Centre for Design was asked by Public Health Agency Northern Ireland to reimagine conditions along the river. How could we use design to lift an area associated with poor emotional wellbeing? How could we encourage local residents to turn the banks and bridges of the river into a more lively and lived-in place?

The sheer scale of the project, named Our Future Foyle, was daunting. It encompassed so many challenging dimensions. So, we began as we always do – by engaging local communities along the River Foyle in a conversation about their future. One of our ideas for community engagement was to build a giant wooden replica of a whale called Dopey Dick, which famously swam up the river in 1977 and provided some shared communal relief at the height of The Troubles in Northern Ireland. Our replica whale repeated the trip up the river as part of Derry's annual Maritime Festival and Halloween celebrations, becoming a focal point for co-design events with different groups.

Our research team then placed a series of temporary interactive installations along the riverfront over the course of four days. These installations were produced in partnership with artists, musicians and students from Queen's University in Belfast. More than 15,000 people in local communities viewed what was happening.

Gradually, we built up a clear picture of local perceptions of the area and developed a strategy for suicide prevention with the potential to revitalise the riverfront and address the mental health of the communities that occupy its space. This approach was conceived with a number of elements designed to combine physical barriers and soft barriers with an increased footfall along the river. Four ideas were taken forward to development, named Foyle Reeds, Foyle Bubbles, Foyle Experience and Foyle Aware.

Foyle Reeds is an art installation that engages with a redesign of the main bridge to create a physical suicide barrier. The bridge is exposed to the elements due to its span and height.

Through consultation, the research team found that local people felt uncomfortable crossing the bridge due to its lack of protection from wind and rain. The protective design is based on the natural reeds that occur in the landscape around the site – it will be deployed on the 864-metre-long bridge to deter jumpers without imprisoning people in prison-like bars or cages and reinforcing the stigma around suicide.

Community engagement: local people learn about the project inside a giant wooden replica of a whale which was spotted in the river in 1977

Foyle Bubbles along the riverfront are designed to animate public space while providing opportunities for local social entrepreneurs

The Foyle Reeds installation will combine the visual language of the local fauna with interactive lighting so that 12,000 digital reeds change in colour and brightness as people walk along, creating an appealing sensory experience. People will have the opportunity to feel a sense of ownership towards the installation – they can adopt a reed for a small payment and change its colour and brightness using a special app on their smartphone. Foyle Reeds has the capacity to turn the bridge into a landmark, creating a visual icon to which the community can relate. It will also be the largest art installation in Northern Ireland.

Foyle Bubbles comprises a series of satellite spaces designed to house arts, commercial, educational and wellbeing activities around the riverfront; these will act as soft barriers and increase footfall, so achieving natural surveillance of the site. These portable pods will provide opportunities for enterprise and community services, from selling coffee or cutting hair to giving citizens' advice. Individuals and organisations occupying the pods will undertake mandatory mental health training in return for reduced rent. This mechanism will mean that mental health support and counselling can be available each day, without becoming too overt or clinical.

The portability of the 42 pop-up pods will be key to their success as they can respond to

View of Foyle Bubbles framing the Peace Bridge: the operators of these portable pods will offer mental health support to the community

negative spots along the riverfront by moving into areas with low footfall, anti-social behaviour or poor-quality lighting. Local people will be able to run a Foyle Bubble just as they can sponsor a Foyle Reed. These two high-profile interventions will be complemented by Foyle Experience, which will build a series of sensory spaces along the river for contemplation and reflection, and Foyle Aware, a media campaign looking at suicide prevention and mental health awareness.

In 2018, Our Future Foyle moved from research and feasibility to planning and delivery of the key design interventions, as identified in the study. A new non-profit vehicle was established by the government in Northern Ireland to obtain more than £25 million in infrastructure investment to

achieve significant health, tourism and economic benefits for the city and the wider region. Researchers Ralf Alwani and Jak Spencer moved to Derry to set up a design studio, Urban Scale Interventions, to work on the new inclusive design strategy for the riverfront.

Our Future Foyle is now a flagship part of a comprehensive programme to rejuvenate the entire area. It shows the power of community engagement and creative design research to translate local anxieties into tangible interventions for change. Importantly, it demonstrates a community-based response to suicide risk rather than dependence on formal health services. Its scale and ambition are what makes this project stand out – a river designed for everyone.

top
Concept image for the Foyle Reeds, which will be the largest public art installation in Northern Ireland

middle
Architect Ralf Alwani tests a set of prototype Foyle Reeds

right
Local people will be able to alter the colour and intensity of the Foyle Reeds on the bridge from their smartphone

Scooter

The motorised mobility scooter has undoubtedly transformed the lives of millions of people with disabilities. It is a practical and utilitarian response to difficulties with walking over long distances. But it also carries a stigma – it can only be used by one person, which is unhelpful to social interaction with others, and it can be hard to store away. Many mobility scooters are parked outside the home by their users, signalling that a frail and vulnerable person lives there. Could the mobility scooter be reimagined as a more desirable and flexible object, one that connects with others and doesn't stereotype the person using it as old or weak?

I learnt about the drawbacks and limitations of mobility scooters when the Helen Hamlyn Centre for Design worked with the design firm Priestman Goode on a brief to create a new product or service that could keep people on the move as they aged. This was a commission for an exhibition called *New Old* at the Design Museum, which I was curating. We organised a forum of older people to hear their views. The design team, led by Paul Priestman, quickly latched onto the idea of the push scooter as an inclusive mode of transport now ubiquitous in family life, popular with both children and parents. The trouble is that, at some stage, people stop using them. You rarely see seniors whizzing around on a push scooter.

Paul Priestman's response was to design a 'Scooter for Life' which adapts over the user's lifespan as their mobility requirements evolve. The idea was to offer older people greater independence without the stigma associated with the mobility scooter. The concept reclaims the push scooter for older people by designing a three-wheeled version to provide stability. A large front basket serves as a shopping trolley, allowing users to take their slim-profile scooter into shops as well as their own homes. A small seat and electric motor can be added to the scooter if foot power becomes difficult. Grandparents are able to share the same universal activity with their grandchildren.

The Scooter for Life concept promotes independence among older and disabled people by tackling the 'last mile', the distance one has to travel from a bus stop or a railway station in order to get home. Digital technology can be incorporated into the scooter in order to map uneven sections of pavement or facilitate a 'take me home' function, helping those with mild dementia. A prototype was built for the *New Old* exhibition, which was seen by 80,000 people at the Design Museum in London in 2017 before visiting Taiwan, Poland and New York. Priestman Goode continues to negotiate with manufacturers to bring this innovation to market.

Product form of the Scooter for Life: designed for stability and social inclusion

left

Scooter for Life by Priestman Goode, 2017: the mobility scooter reimagined as an inclusive mode of transport that bridges generations

below

Sketch by Paul Priestman shows how the Scooter for Life can adapt for each stage of life

The scooter is conceived to be an unobtrusive lifestyle accessory when out and about

Stairlift

Researcher Ross Atkin (right) talks to a stairlift user as part of the connected stairlift project

Up. Down. Up. Down. The stairlift is a curious artefact, and controversial too. Dismissed by some as an intrusive and stigmatising piece of engineering that screams disability at its users, it is championed by others as a lifeline for people with mobility impairments who wish to live independently in their own home. It also provides reassurance to the owner's friends and family that their loved one is safe when moving between floors.

But what if that reassurance could be extended by digitally enabling the stairlift, turning it from a dumb conveyor of people and goods into a smart service? That was the question we asked when we worked with Stannah Stairlifts, a family-owned business in the field. Our project looked at how a digital network of care could be built around the movements of a stairlift in the home. The big idea was that each time a connected stairlift moved, it could automatically send messages to designated family and friends – a tweet from Grandma to the grandchildren, for example, telling them she was up and moving about as usual.

The study asked three essential questions: is digital monitoring a useful addition to a stairlift? What kind of monitoring is acceptable to older people? And what is the appropriate way to deliver information to their informal care network? We learnt a lot from the research, building up insights through user scenarios which confirmed that the stairlift was indeed a suitable location for remote monitoring technology (along with the kettle and the refrigerator, but *not* the toilet flush).

We went on to develop a fully working system with Stannah's technical team and we tested it with seven stairlift users in the south of England. The new system was installed in their homes as well as on the smartphones of relatives. The system generates alerts if the stairlift user is inactive for a long period, prompting the circle of caregivers to check on them. In addition, it manages information flow between different members of the care network, helping them to co-ordinate support.

The project, entitled Rise, resulted in a new connected stairlift for the digital age, which was then taken by Stannah into a full commercial pilot. The company was so encouraged by the results of a people-centred approach to innovation that it commissioned a second project. This looked more broadly at how older people at risk from falling on

Researcher Shruti Grover (left) studies posture and balance with a female participant in her project to develop ways to stop women falling in the home

the stairs could be better supported to stay active and independent in their homes.

Through research, we learnt that women aged over 55 often fall due to a decline in balance and gait over a number of years, more so than men. This is something that can be hard to measure or to visualise, making it difficult to track any decline. People can measure and control their weight gain using weighing scales, but nothing equivalent exists to measure a loss of balance and an increase in dizziness that may lead to a fall. So we decided to design an intervention which allows people to measure their balance as they would their weight.

The result of our research was a smartphone app, Balance, which provides a diagnostic test of

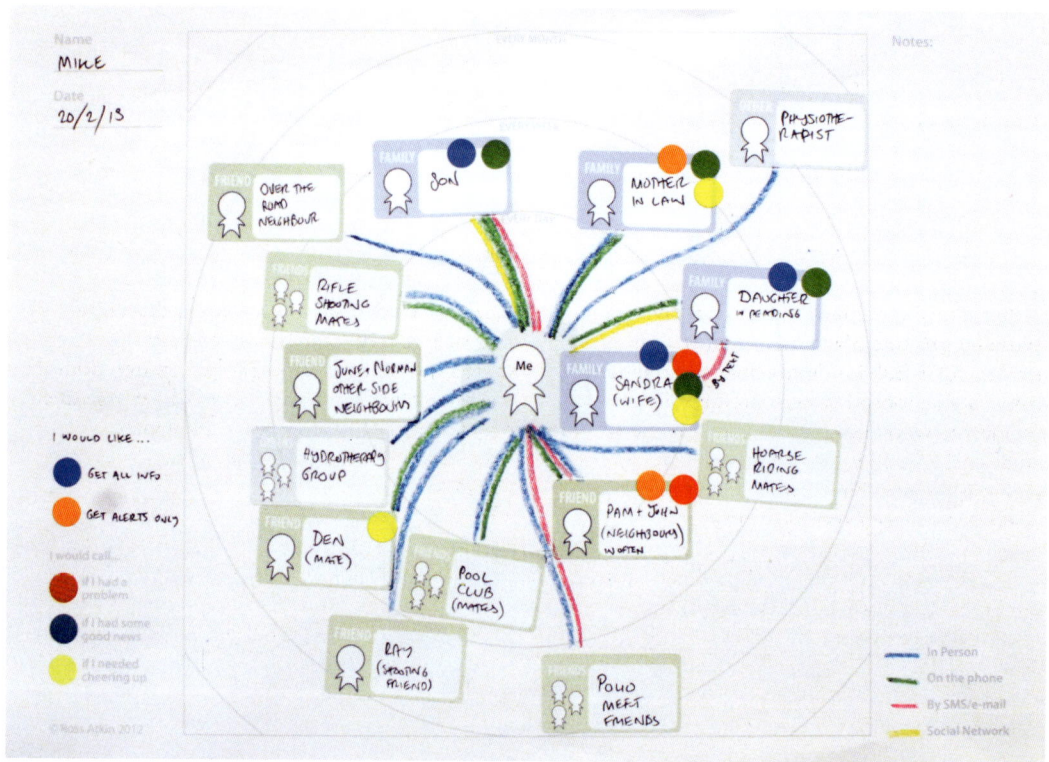

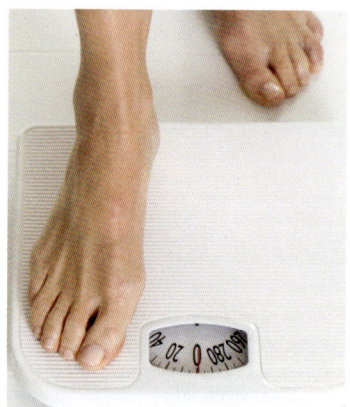
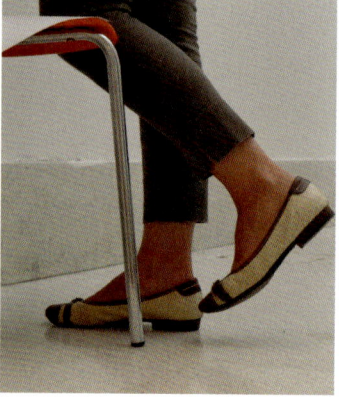

above

A participant in the connected stairlift study sketches out their circle of care: drawing and mapping techniques are frequently used in Helen Hamlyn Centre for Design projects

left

The aim of the Balance project was to make measuring balance as easy as measuring weight

static posture based on four scientific factors. This test can be easily completed by an individual in the home. Once the test is finished, the application provides tips on improving posture and directs the user to appropriate exercise videos to support better balance. Stannah has commercially developed the app. It is rare to find a manufacturer that not only enhances its core product, as in the connected stairlift, but simultaneously seeks to reduce human reliance on it.

Street

It's no coincidence that many of the most important principles and projects of inclusive design have been played out in public – in the built environment. Our streets are supposed to be shared by all, but their design and planning often exclude people with disabilities or the frailties that come with ageing. Several of our projects have addressed the question of how to create a more equitable streetscape for everyone.

The way in which older and disabled people are depicted on British street signs is itself revealing. There have been frequent calls to replace or update the universal pictogram for disability, created in 1969 by the Danish designer Susanne Koefoed, which depicts a passive upright figure in a wheelchair. Campaigners want a more active image showing the disabled person leaning forward to propel the wheelchair themselves. The elderly persons road sign used only in the UK is even more stigmatising – a sad silhouette of a stooping couple with a walking stick.

In 2007, we worked with a design team at Wolff Olins on a project to create a public awareness campaign to encourage both greater awareness

The Go Steady campaign by a design team at Wolff Olins, winner of the 2007 DBA Inclusive Design Challenge

Concept drawing showing 'access ribbons' to improve access for pedestrians and cyclists around transport interchanges: Fiona Scott, 2003

of the mobility challenges that people face, and a desire to help. Only five per cent of people are wheelchair users and many disabilities which affect mobility are invisible. The Go Steady campaign aimed to signal vulnerability in a subtle way that would elicit empathy and action. At the centre of the campaign was a symbol of an arrow and half-arrow which suggests the 'm' for mobility and also a helping hand. The symbol was designed to be used in a wide range of applications – on posters and products related to mobility, as well as on bus passes and medical notes to signal that a person might have issues with balance and falling. The Go Steady campaign won the 2007 DBA Inclusive Design Challenge.

Changing attitudes to disability on the streets is one thing. Redesigning the streetscape itself to improve access is another. In 2010, we were asked by the UK government body on urban design, CABE (Commission for Architecture and the Built Environment – now part of the Design Council), to investigate why a new concept in street design – 'shared space' – was proving such a serious challenge for people with visual impairments. Shared space was pioneered in the Netherlands by a traffic engineer, Hans Monderman. It sought to minimise the segregation between different modes of road use by removing familiar markers such as kerbs and railings.

However, despite the democratic aim to turn streets back into places for walkers and cyclists, and not just as conduits for cars, the shared space approach unwittingly excluded people with sight loss. These were individuals who relied on kerbs and railings to navigate the street environment – they could not negotiate with vehicles by line of sight and found the uncertainty over who had priority to be unsettling. Disability charities protested long and loud over the introduction of shared space schemes in London.

Our research built up a picture of how visually impaired people use environmental cues to navigate the street. We conducted street surveys and an ethnographic study involving eight people making local journeys. This was followed by a series of proposals for how street design practice could better include the needs of people with sight loss. The project generated national guidance on such subjects as street furniture and tactile paving, as well as an innovative proposal to help the visually impaired to navigate unpredictable and troublesome temporary obstructions caused by roadworks.

In a separate study which also addressed the different needs of street users, we worked with architects Scott Brownrigg to look at the streets around transport interchanges, which are often characterless and confusing. Using London's Stratford East transport interchange as a case study, we proposed a series of 'access ribbons' designed for pedestrians and cyclists to penetrate the neighbourhood, enhancing personal journeys between the interchange and the surrounding district for walkers and wheelchair users.

One of our earliest projects as a research centre, in 2001, was a campaign to encourage local neighbourhood walking as a regular exercise to reduce the risk of heart disease; this involved placing posters next to bus stops saying, 'What are you waiting for?' and redesigning local maps in a circular bullseye format to measure distance by walking time rather than miles. Today, the evolving state of our streets continues to challenge the practice of inclusive design.

Campaign for the British Heart Foundation encouraging local neighbourhood walking: Ellie Risdale, 2001

DESIGNING A WORLD FOR EVERYONE

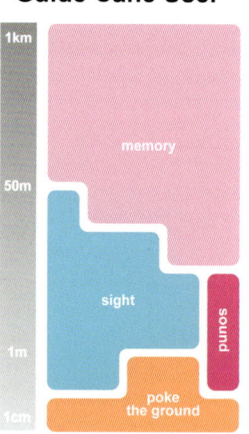
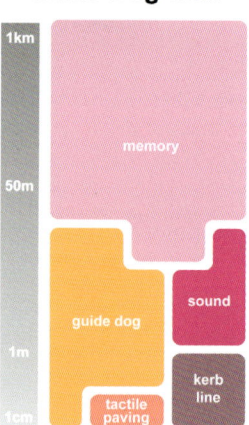
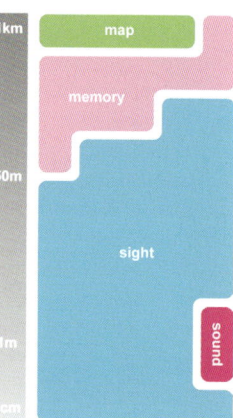

top
Diagram shows how different street users navigate space from 1 cm to 1 km: Sight Line project, 2011

middle
Diagram by Ross Atkin showing how kerbs, railings and tactile paving are essential to enable people with sight loss to navigate the street environment

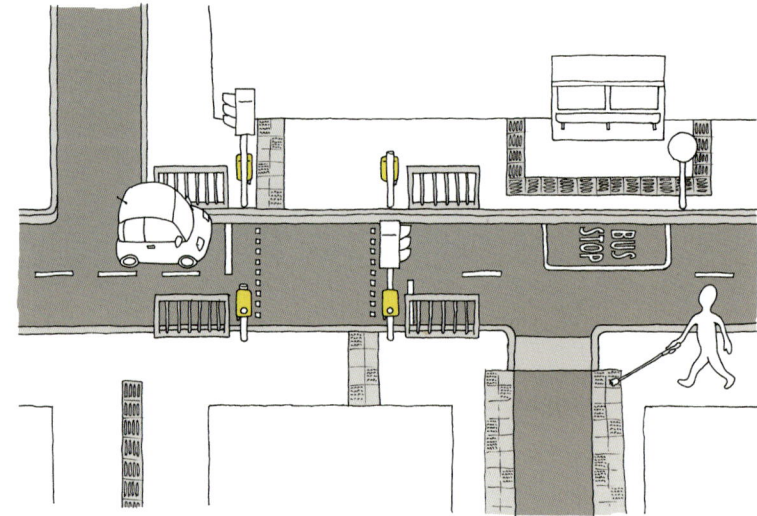

bottom
Concept design by Ross Atkin for a new system of temporary roadwork barriers

right
Research participant observed during a study to explore how visually impaired people navigate local streets

Taxi

The London Black Cab is not just a global icon but also one of the few purpose-built taxis in the world. However, by 2013, its familiar and much admired design was over 20 years old and in need of modernisation. London was also looking at ambitious new carbon reduction targets, and a low-emission taxi became a target for policy-makers.

Our own interest in the taxi was in making it more inclusive for all ages and abilities.

All these things came together in a project with the Royal College of Art's Vehicle Design department, along with automotive manufacturer Karsan and design studio Hexagon, both of which are based in Turkey. The objective: to design a

Redesigning an icon: model of an inclusive new London taxi for the 21st century

The new London taxi pays close attention to driver ergonomics

new London taxi for the 21st century. Through a 'deep dive' programme of interviews with taxi drivers and passengers, visits to taxi ranks, taxi shelters, service centres and trade shows, online forums and physical observations, we identified opportunities for change. Our research team took one of Karsan's existing prototype vehicles, with a large, airy interior that is lightweight in construction, and used it as the basis for the creative exploration of exterior design, driver space and passenger space.

The study concentrated on inclusivity from the perspective of both taxi drivers and passengers. The taxi is the driver's workspace where they spend long hours, but the driver environment did not provide the necessary comfort and amenities. As one taxi driver told us in typically forthright fashion: 'Show me a London cabbie and I'll show you someone with a back, neck, leg or shoulder problem.' In contrast, passengers only spend a short time in the cab and therefore have different physical, mental, visual and cognitive needs.

Central to the study was a co-creation workshop where participants critiqued a real cab and explored solutions. The inclusive taxi design that resulted sought to make the driver area more comfortable and functional while increasing flexibility in the passenger environment on short journeys; it incorporated a new driver interface with new technology, addressed the door aperture to improve passenger access, and sought to create an iconic new exterior look – important for both drivers and tourists.

The results of our design study were unveiled at a London taxi showcase in January 2014 at which the Mayor of London, Boris Johnson, announced that all new cabs presented for licensing in the capital should be zero emission-capable by 2018. We subsequently continued to develop many aspects of the new taxi design with Karsan and its design team, Studio Hexagon. This flagship project is widely cited today for providing design guidelines on how to create a truly inclusive taxi.

left, *top*
Concept for illuminated signs to aid passenger safety on exiting the vehicle

left, *bottom*
Headlamp detail for the iconic new taxi exterior

right, *top*
Concept diagram communicates the scope of the project

right, *bottom*
Test rigs were constructed to test access for passengers of all ages and abilities

TAXI

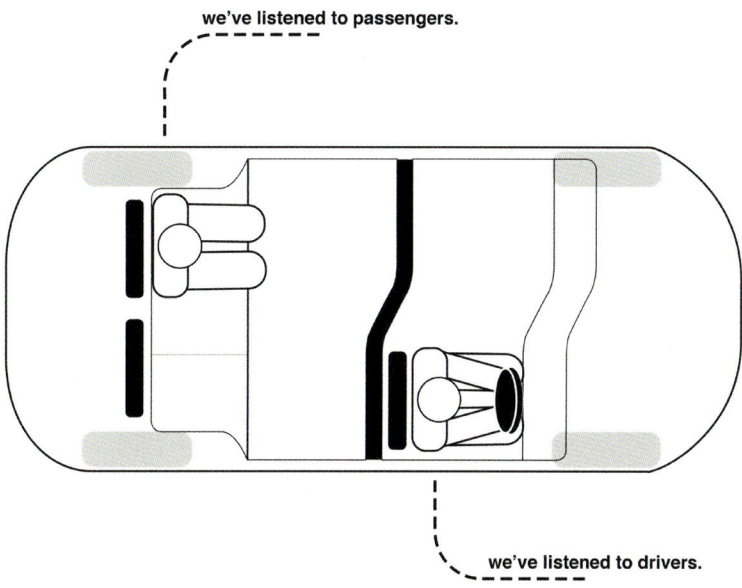

we've listened to passengers.

we've listened to drivers.

117

Typeface

Read Regular, Natasha Frensch, 2003: typeface by a dyslexic designer for dyslexics

There are nearly three million severely dyslexic individuals in Britain who struggle with reading, writing and spelling; people with dyslexia may sometimes describe 'letters dancing off the page'. For a long time, the focus of assistive research in the field centred on computer software, particularly for children, and relatively little attention was paid to type design. But one student project at the Royal College of Art changed all that.

In 2002, Dutch designer and typographer Natasha Frensch, who is herself dyslexic, decided to explore the relationship between dyslexia and typography. On graduation, she joined the Helen Hamlyn Centre for Design as a Research Associate to develop her master's project – a typeface for dyslexics, supported by the Audi Design Foundation. She began by experimenting with hand-drawn letterforms that were independent in character and could be easily distinguished from each other by dyslexics, while also forming a cohesive alphabet.

The conventional process in type design is to create an alphabet derived from just a few characters. Frensch, however, chose a completely different approach in order to prevent confusion between the letters b and d, p and q, f and t, m and n, and so on, which is common among dyslexics. Early in the study, she realised how a typeface designed by a dyslexic for other dyslexics could assist them and increase their motivation to read. A decision was made to concentrate on a sans serif typeface to ensure the objective of reducing form and detail, with the inner forms of the letters kept large and open.

The project developed through a programme of user research co-ordinated at the RCA with around 100 dyslexic children and adults, from which a new typeface emerged. This was then exhaustively tested against conventional typefaces, amended and improved. Positive test results encouraged her to persevere with the project and consult leading European type designers for advice on how to integrate unique letterforms into a consistent sans serif typeface. The work led to the introduction of three new typefaces in the Read type family: Read Regular, Read Smallcaps and Read Space, a specially spaced version for younger children.

Frensch wrote and produced a limited edition book in English and Dutch to explain the development of the new typeface, and created a website (www.readregular.com) to promote it to a wider educational audience. Agreement was reached with a number of publishing houses who wished to use her typeface for children's books. Today, the project continues to have relevance: it is estimated that around a quarter of all Royal College of Art students have some form of dyslexia.

Vehicle

From stories of flying carpets to science fiction movies, autonomous vehicles have always gripped the imagination. Some of that fascination is located in fear – self-governing machines might go out of control – and some of it is about a sense of awe at what is now possible. Today, as vehicle technology begins its biggest transformation since the invention of the internal combustion engine, driverless cars are opening up new possibilities for inclusive mobility – irrespective of age, ability or economic background.

A driverless car, when used in conjunction with other transport modes, could, for instance, help create a mobility network that is truly door-to-door, solving the problem of the 'last mile' of the journey for those with walking difficulties. Autonomous ambulances could support patient transport and discharge. Driverless community vehicles could bring much-needed services into the neighbourhood and to a user's doorstep. Rural and low-income communities with low levels of private car ownership might benefit in particular.

Autonomous vehicle concept for the London Borough of Greenwich GATEway project, 2018. In this scenario, you can dial up a mobile office that drives over and picks you up, wherever you are

VEHICLE

Autonomous vehicle concept turns the daily commute into a cappuccino-and-croissant experience

We investigated people's hopes, fears and aspirations around autonomous vehicles as part of a project in the London Borough of Greenwich led by the Transport Research Laboratory. This focused on the GATEway Shuttle, a prototype vehicle that can hold up to four passengers without a driver operating it. Through a series of co-creation workshops with experts, an RCA research team created utopian and dystopian scenarios for the future of driverless cars. The project then went on to develop vehicle concepts with students to flesh out these scenarios.

While autonomous vehicles are one part of the future of mobility, electric vehicles represent another. Early in the development of this vehicle typology, we worked with Norwegian electric car company TH!NK to anticipate how a 'connected car' using digital technology might reinvent the relationship between the driver, the vehicle and the city. The study investigated the potential for the electric vehicle to become a mobile information interface, offering services that go beyond anything a petrol or diesel car might offer.

A digitally connected parked car might, for example, switch on to provide street lighting for passers-by, act as a wi-fi hotspot, advertise local shops or even point a lost tourist in the right direction. It might also be preheated and defrosted from the home. A digitally connected car on the road might communicate with other vehicles, letting other people know its location and estimated time of arrival. As part of the study, we built in-depth profiles of potential electric car users and created an interface that adapts to different situations and drivers, displaying information only when required.

Our research into autonomous and electric vehicles echoed earlier studies in which our

Driverless vehicle system designed by Merih Kunur. Mobilicity project, 2004

researchers investigated new forms of mobility that could reduce environmental impact and over-reliance on the private car. In 2000, Research Associate Shaun Hutchinson partnered with Ford to present a new hybrid model of public–private urban mobility for 2030, in response to a desire to price cars out of city centres. One scenario showed the customer buying a package of road miles that could be redeemed via different forms of transport, rather than a single vehicle.

In 2004, Merih Kunur's Mobilicity project presented a shared system of large, driverless vehicles that could pick up passengers on demand, forming a road train to traverse the city. Based on research in London, Istanbul and Hong Kong, Mobilicity was developed by an industrial consortium led by Capoco Design. In 2005, researcher Serge Porcher explored the use of rear-screen digital projection technologies for the car dashboard in a project with Visteon. A model of the work was presented at the Geneva Motor Show.

Behind each of these projects was a commitment to make mobility more inclusive for diverse users, especially those with the frailties and disabilities of age. We also designed road safety campaigns for older drivers, encouraging them to take an eye test or speak to their doctor if they felt they might be unsafe on the road. Today, as digital and battery technologies reinvent the motor car, some of our speculations are becoming a reality.

VEHICLE

top
Ford vehicle concept for 2030: Shaun Hutchinson, 2001

middle
Electric car driver profile compiled for a TH!NK project

bottom
Sketch concepts for Norwegian electric car company TH!NK by Filip Krnja

123

above

Model of a rear screen projection system for a car dashboard, shown at the Geneva Motor Show by Visteon: Serge Porcher, 2005

left

Arcadian autonomous vehicle concept inspired by an eight-year-old who wanted her pet to pick her up from school everyday

Campaign with Guide Dogs to encourage older drivers to take an eye test based on the language of car registration plates: Gero Grundman, 2004

VEHICLE

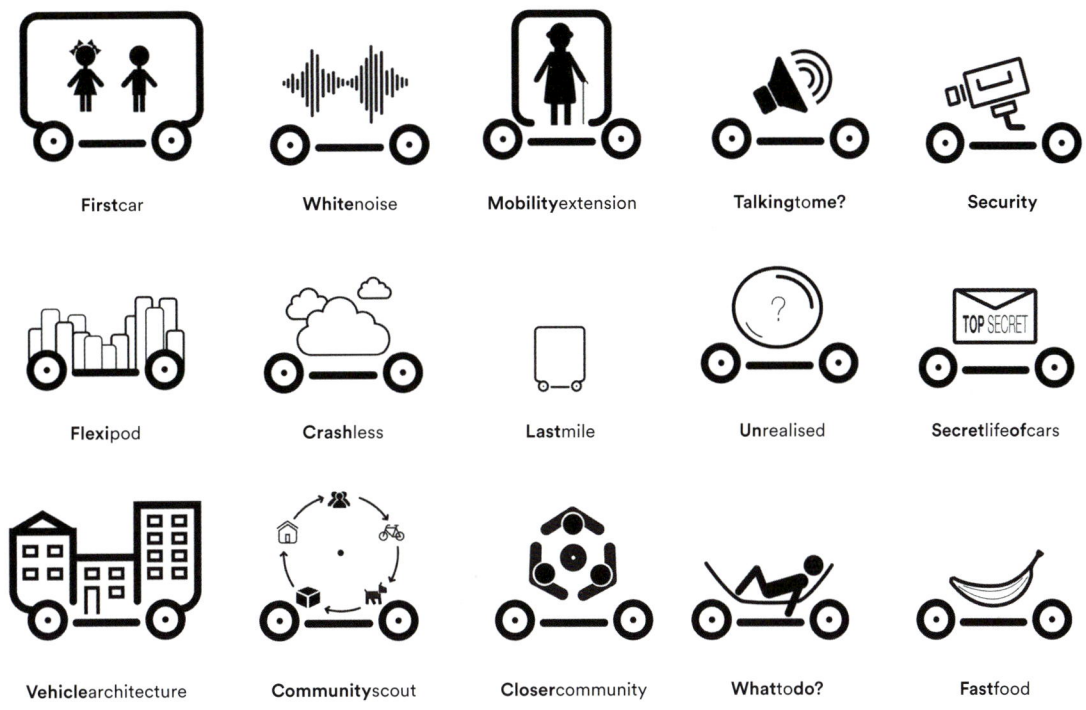

Graphic by Samuel Johnson and Dan Quinlan imagines a range of different uses for driverless vehicles

Road safety campaign for older drivers: Jean-Paul Baptiste, 2007

Wheelchair

Morph folding wheel makes wheelchairs more portable: Duncan Fitzsimons, 2007

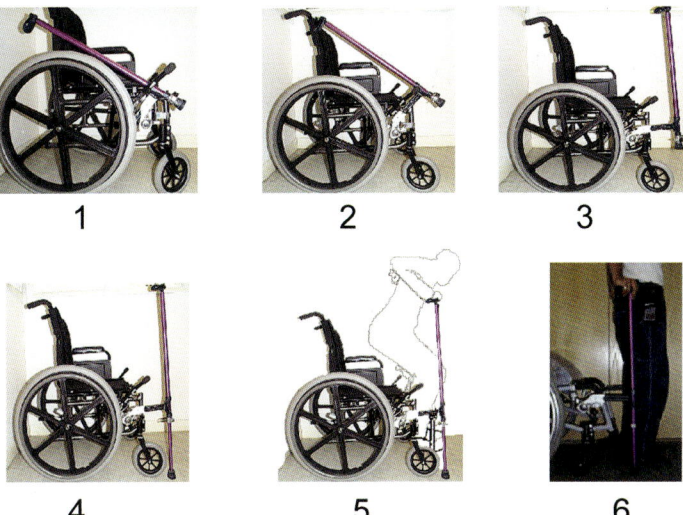

Abilizer wheelchair-mounted system enables wheelchair users to stand and balance: Judith Anderson, 2000

It is entirely fitting that this survey of 30 everyday artefacts and environments that the Helen Hamlyn Centre for Design has sought to influence over the past 30 years should conclude with the wheelchair. This is the ultimate symbol of disability – but also an object of innovation and ingenuity in recent times.

Inspired by the work of David Constantine, the wheelchair design pioneer who founded the charity Motivation and is himself a Royal College of Art graduate, our research community has looked at the wheelchair from several angles. A common theme has been the desire to give wheelchair users the same opportunities in the social and built environment as everyone else, in an era when the number of people using wheelchairs is growing rapidly.

To aid mobility and freedom of movement for older and disabled people, wheelchairs that fold are now more common. But there's a problem: many folding wheelchairs are not that portable. The degree to which they can fold down is restricted by the size of the wheel, which makes the wheelchair a bulky and awkward item to store during travel. This problem was successfully addressed with the world's first foldable wheelchair wheel, developed by design engineer Duncan Fitzsimons, a student winner of a Helen Hamlyn Design Award in 2007.

Using this detachable wheel, a wheelchair can, for the first time, be folded up, allowing it to be stored easily at home, in the boot of a small car, or in an overhead locker on an aeroplane. Fitzsimons first developed his foldable wheelchair wheel for other students – to enable bicycles to be stored more easily in the hallways of cramped student accommodation. But we soon advised him to redirect its application to the wheelchair market. Fitzsimons later teamed up with Maddak, a US-based manufacturing company, to make his patent-protected invention widely available, claiming that the collapsible wheel is 'the last piece in the puzzle for the folding wheelchair'.

Giving wheelchair users the same access to mobility is one form of equality of opportunity. Providing the ability for them to stand and balance out of their wheelchair in social situations is another. People in wheelchairs are often placed at a disadvantage in social gatherings as they are seated at a lower level and out of the sightline of others. One of the first graduate projects to be developed on our Helen Hamlyn Research Associates programme in 2000 was Judith Anderson's Abilizer, a wheelchair-mounted system that enables wheelchair users to stand and balance.

Tilting trike can be pedalled by hand by children without lower body strength: Ben Wilson, 2002

There are compelling clinical reasons why disabled people should have the facility to stand up out of their wheelchair: to aid digestion, maintain muscle elasticity, relieve pelvic pressure and improve blood circulation, for example. But beyond that, there is the social need to avoid the feelings of isolation and exclusion associated with being at a different height when interacting with non-wheelchair users. The Abilizer, first developed with a group of paraplegics at Salisbury District Hospital, provided a fully working prototype with wide application for many different groups of wheelchair users.

The needs of children have not been forgotten in our focus on wheelchairs. One of our most memorable and satisfying projects was with children's charity Whizz-Kidz to develop a pedal-powered tricycle for children that could be quickly adapted to the needs of those without lower body strength. We learnt that many young people with limited mobility feel stigmatised using a traditional wheelchair when going to play outside with other children – they wanted a pedal vehicle with the same level of design style and 'street' credibility as everyone else's bikes.

RCA design graduate Ben Wilson, a specialist in contemporary cycle design, came up with a brilliant solution. He developed a street-smart tilting trike that could be swiftly reconfigured from a foot pedal-powered vehicle to one pedalled by hand, using modular, ready-made bicycle components. It also incorporated a unique steering mechanism

that enabled the user to steer by redistributing their body weight. Two vehicles resulted from the project – one in aluminium, the other in stainless steel. These were tested with a mix of children of different abilities. So cool and stylish was the tilting trike – and so exhilarating was the ride – that everyone wanted to own one, irrespective of their physical ability.

Developing the tilting trike was inclusive design in action, bringing everyone onto the same playing field through empathic research, creative experiment and technical application. In its own way, it sums up everything the Helen Hamlyn Centre for Design has tried to achieve in its projects spanning three decades.

Project Credits

Airport

Process to Pleasure

Helen Hamlyn Research Associates Programme 2000–2003

- Research Associates: Karen Adcock, Samson Adjei, Pascal Anson, Carl Turner
- Research Team: Nigel Coates, Alma Erlich, Jeremy Myerson, John Smith, Raymond Turner
- Research Partner: British Airports Authority (BAA)

Ambulance

Redesigning the Emergency Ambulance

Special Research Project 2010–2011

- Lead Researchers: Ed Matthews, Dale Harrow
- Research Associates: Gianpaolo Fusari, Yusuf Muhammad
- Research Partners: Imperial College St Mary's NHS Trust; Vehicle Design Department, RCA (Royal College of Art); Department of Emergency Medicine, University of the West of England; London Ambulance Service
- Funded by: London NHS (Regional Innovation Fund) and Helen Hamlyn Trust

Bank

Hybrid Space Making

Helen Hamlyn Research Associates Programme 2015–2016

- Research Associate: Andrew Thompson
- Research Team: Imogen Privett, Jeremy Myerson (RCA); Philip Ross, Owen King (UnWork); Klaus Sandbiller (UniCredit)
- Research Partner: UniCredit

Bathroom

Safe and Sensual

Helen Hamlyn Research Associates Programme

- Mary Wagstaff (2002–2003) with Hansgrohe

Watergate

- Barnaby Barford (2003) with ESL Industries

Indulgent Bathing

- Julie Mathias (2005) with Ideal Standard and Studio Levien
- Tomek Rygalik (2006–2007) with Ideal Standard and Studio Levien

Beer Glass

The Ultimate Pint Glass

Innovation Project 2009–2010

PROJECT CREDITS

- Research Team: Sarah Douglas, Chris McGinley, Caroline Till
- Project Lead: Jeremy Myerson, member, Design and Technology Alliance Against Crime, Home Office
- Lead Partner: Design Council
- Design Partner: Design Bridge

Bus Stop

Is That My Bus?

Design Business Association Inclusive Design Challenge Commended Entry 2005

- Research Lead: Julia Cassim
- Design Team: Lacock Gullam
- Research Partner: Design Business Association

Care Home

Design and Dementia

Helen Hamlyn Research Associates Programme 2009–2011

- Research Associates: Gregor Timlin, Nick Rysenbry, Ying Jiang
- Research Lead: Rama Gheerawo
- Research Partner: Bupa

Togetherness

Helen Hamlyn Research Associates Programme 2013–2014

- Research Associate: Lisa Johansson
- Research Partner: Kinnarps

Ageing the Vertical City

Special Research Project, Hong Kong, 2017

- Project Directors: Rama Gheerawo, Sean Donahue
- Project Manager: Masashi Kajita
- Project Team: Sidse Carroll, Gabriele Meldaikyte, Elizabeth Roberts, Samantha Yang
- Research Partner: Hong Kong Polytechnic University
- Sponsor: Debbie Lo Creativity Foundation

Classroom

Lighting for Learning

Helen Hamlyn Research Associates Programme 2013–2014

- Research Associate: Amanda Buckley
- Research Partner: Megaman Charity Trust Fund

Concentrate

Helen Hamlyn Research Associates Programme 2003

- Research Associate: Mark Champkins
- Research Partner: MAK Architects

Crutch

Pro-Crutches

Helen Hamlyn Research Associates Programme 2002

- Research Associate: Guy Robinson
- Research Partner: Audi Design Foundation

Desk

Work at Home

Research Project 1999

- Research Team: Daniel Charny, Alma Erlich
- Research Partner: Leonard Cheshire

Home/Work

Helen Hamlyn Research Associates Programme 2004

- Research Associates: Peter Fullager and Dan Jones
- Research Partner: Dams International

Playground

Helen Hamlyn Research Associates Programme 2000

- Research Associate: Lotta Vaanenen
- Research Partner: Leonard Cheshire

Head in the Sky

New Old Exhibition Special Commission 2017

- Designer: Konstantin Grcic
- Curator: Jeremy Myerson
- Research Partner: The Design Museum

Food Pack

A Jar We Can Open

Helen Hamlyn Student Design Award Winner 1994

- Designer: Gavin Pryke
- Industry Partners: Rockware Glass; Safeway

Opening Up

Helen Hamlyn Research Associates Programme 2002

- Research Associates: Edward Goodwin, Richard Hartshorn
- Research Partner: Waitrose

On a Plate

Helen Hamlyn Research Associates Programme 2004

- Research Associate: Katherine Gough
- Research Partner: Marks & Spencer

Milkman

BA Inclusive Design Challenge Winner 2000

- Research Lead: Julia Cassim
- Design Team: Factory Design
- Research Partner: Design Business Association

Garden

Green Spaces

Design for Autism Research Programme 2012

- PhD Researcher: Katie Gaudion
- Senior Research Associate: Chris McGinley
- PhD Supervisors: Jeremy Myerson, Ashley Hall
- Research Consultant: Colum Lowe, Being
- Research Partner: The Kingwood Trust

PROJECT CREDITS

Garment

Impact Wave

Helen Hamlyn Research Associates Programme 2000

- Research Associate: Dan Plant
- Research Partner: Levi Strauss

Smart Wearables

DBA Inclusive Design Challenge, shortlisted entry 2002

- Research Lead: Julia Cassim
- Design Team: Pearlfisher
- Research Partner: Design Business Association

Aura Power Suit

New Old Exhibition Special Commission 2017

- Designer: Yves Behar, Fuseproject
- Curator: Jeremy Myerson
- Research Partner: The Design Museum

Hospital

Carecentre

Design Out Medical Error (DOME) Research Programme 2008–2012

- Principal Investigator: Jeremy Myerson
- Researchers: Grace Davey, Jonathan West
- Research Partners: EPSRC; Department of Surgery and Cancer, Imperial College London; Imperial College Business School

Resus:station

Special Research Project 2005

- Research Lead: Roger Coleman

- Designers: Sally Halls and Jonathan West
- Research Partners: Imperial College London School of Medicine; NHS National Patient Safety Agency

Design Bugs Out

Demonstrator Projects 2009

- Researchers: Grace Davey, Jonathan West
- Research Partners: Design Council; NHS Purchasing and Supply Agency
- Funded by: Department of Health

Design for Patient Dignity

Demonstrator Projects 2010

- Researchers: Maja Kecman, Yusuf Muhammad, Karina Torlei
- Research Partner: Design Council
- Funded by: Department of Health

Senso

Future Critical Care Project 2015–2016

- Research Associate: Gabriele Meldaikte
- Senior Research Associate: Gianpaolo Fusari
- Healthcare Research Lead: Jonathan West
- Research Partner: The London Clinic

Violence and Aggression in A&E

Special Research Project 2011

- Research Associate: Gianpaolo Fusari
- Senior Research Associate: Maja Kecman
- Research Partners: PearsonLloyd (lead consultant); Tavistock Institute; Tavistock Consultancy Service; University of the West of England (Academic Department of Emergency Care); University of Bath (School of Management)
- Funded by: Design Council/Department of Health

Necksafe

Special Research Project 2011–2013

- Senior Research Associates: Maja Kecman, Karina Torlei
- Research Lead: Ed Matthews
- Research Partners: Bath Institute of Medical Engineering; Royal National Hospital for Rheumatic Diseases; University of the West of England (Academic Department of Emergency Care); Great Western Ambulance Service; i2R Medical
- Funded by: National Institute for Health Research

Redesigning Surgical Tools

Helen Hamlyn Research Associates Programme 2007

- Research Associates: Maja Kecman and Lisa Stroux
- Research Partners: DePuy Johnson & Johnson

Kitchen

Hand Healthy

Helen Hamlyn Research Associates Programme 2014

- Research Associate: Simon Kinneir
- Research Partner: Arthritis Research UK

Factory Wares

DBA Inclusive Design Challenge Joint Winner 2004

- Research Lead: Julia Cassim
- Design Team: Factory Design
- Research Partner: Design Business Association

Inclusive Konro

Helen Hamlyn Research Associates Programme 2004

- Research Associate: Chris McGinley
- Research Partner: Osaka Gas

Light

light.urban.landscape

Helen Hamlyn Research Associates Programme 2002

- Research Associate: Harry Dobbs
- Research Partner: Targetti

B*light*ed Landscapes

Helen Hamlyn Research Associates Programme 2004

- Research Associate: Matt Dearlove
- Research Partner: Targetti

In The Shade

Helen Hamlyn Research Associates Programme 2011–2012

- Research Associates: Megan Charnley, Tom Jarvis
- Research Partner: Megaman Charity Trust Fund

Medication

Graphic Guidance

Helen Hamlyn Research Associates Programme 2005

- Research Associate: Thea Swayne
- Research Partner: NHS National Patient Safety Agency

PROJECT CREDITS

Packaging Graphics for Injectable Medicines

Helen Hamlyn Research Associates Programme 2007

- Research Associate: Sally Halls
- Research Partner: NHS National Patient Safety Agency

Which Pill When

Helen Hamlyn Research Associates Programme 2004

- Research Associates: Richard Mawle, Chris McGinley
- Research Partner: GlaxoSmithKline

Mobile Phone

'Ello

DBA Inclusive Design Challenge Joint Winner 2004

- Research Lead: Julia Cassim
- Design Team: Seymour Powell
- Research Partner: Design Business Association

Two-Tone Phone

Helen Hamlyn Research Associates Programme 2007

- Research Associates: Matthew Harrison, Cian Plumbe
- Research Partner: BT

Out of the Box

Helen Hamlyn Research Associates Programme 2009

- Research Associates: Clara Gaggero Westaway, Adrian Westaway

- Research Lead: Rama Gheerawo
- Research Partner: Samsung

Chalk

Challenge Workshop, Oslo 2008

- Research Lead: Julia Cassim
- Research Partner: Nokia

Generation Game, Alternative View

Helen Hamlyn Research Associates Programme 2008–2009

- Research Associates: Maja Kecman, Yusuf Muhammad
- Research Partner: Blackberry

The Qualified Self

Helen Hamlyn Research Associates Programme 2013

- Research Associate: Peter Ziegler
- Research Partner: Panasonic

Office

Welcoming Workplace

UK Research Council Project 2006–2008

- Research Team: Jeremy Myerson (Principal Investigator), Jo-Anne Bichard, Catherine Greene, Matthew Harrison, Alma Erlich, John Smith
- Research Partners: Kyushu University, Japan; University of Melbourne, Australia
- Funded by: EPSRC and AHRC

Living Stages/Living Cities

Helen Hamlyn Research Associates Programme 2012–2013

- Research Associates: Imogen Privett, Tom Jarvis
- Research Partners: Haworth, Philips Lighting

Workscapes

Helen Hamlyn Research Associates Programme 2012–2014

- Research Associates: Benjamin Koslowski, Lottie Crumbleholme
- Research Partners: Bossons Group; GlaxoSmithKline; Herman Miller; Plantronics

Park

Inspiration Park

DBA Inclusive Design Challenge Winner 2001

- Research Lead: Julia Cassim
- Design Team: Imagination
- Research Partner: Design Business Association

Power Tool

Power to the People

Helen Hamlyn Research Associates Programme 2001

- Research Associate: Matthew White
- Research Partner: B&Q

Public Toilet

The Great British Public Toilet Map

UK Research Council Project 2012–2014

- Researchers: Jo-Anne Bichard, Gail Ramster
- Research Partner: New Dynamics of Ageing, ESRC
- Funded by: Nominet Trust

River

Our Future Foyle

Special Research Project 2016–2018

- Researchers: Ralf Alwani, Elizabeth Raby
- Research Leads: Jo-Anne Bichard, Jak Spencer, Jonathan West
- Research Partner: Public Health Agency Northern Ireland

Scooter

Scooter for Life

New Old Exhibition Special Commission 2017

- Designer: Priestman Goode
- Creative Team: Paul Priestman, Dan Window, Mike Lambourne
- Curator: Jeremy Myerson
- Research Partner: The Design Museum

Stairlift

Rise

Helen Hamlyn Research Associates Programme 2012–2013

- Research Associate: Ross Atkins
- Research Lead: Rama Gheerawo
- Research Partner: Stannah

Balance on the Go

Helen Hamlyn Research Associates Programme 2014

PROJECT CREDITS

- Research Associates: Shruti Grover, Ross Atkins
- Research Lead: Rama Gheerawo
- Research Partner: Stannah

Street

Go Steady

DBA Inclusive Design Challenge Winner 2007

- Research Lead: Julia Cassim
- Design Team: Wolff Olins
- Research Partner: Design Business Association

Sight Line

Helen Hamlyn Research Associates Programme 2010–2011

- Research Associate: Ross Atkins
- Research Partner: Commission for Architecture and the Built Environment (CABE)

InterchangeABLE

Helen Hamlyn Research Associates Programme 2003

- Research Associate: Fiona Scott
- Research Partner: Scott Brownrigg Architects

Foot Print

Helen Hamlyn Research Associates Programme 2001

- Research Associate: Ellie Risdale
- Research Partner: British Heart Foundation

Taxi

Future London Taxi

Special Research Project 2014–2017

- Project Directors: Rama Gheerawo, Dale Harrow
- Design Team: Helen Fisher, Samuel Johnson, Daniel Quinlan, Elizabeth Roberts, Peter Stevens, Clive Birch, Merih Kunur, Niels van Roij
- Project Manager: Chris McGinley
- Industry Partners: Hexagon; Karsan

Typeface

Read Regular

Helen Hamlyn Research Associates Programme 2003

- Research Associate: Natasha Frensch
- Research Partner: Audi Design Foundation

Vehicle

GATEway

Special Research Project 2016–2018

- Project Directors: Rama Gheerawo, Dale Harrow
- Design Team: Helen Fisher, Samuel Johnson, Daniel Quinlan, Elizabeth Roberts, Gail Ramster, Gabriele Meldaikyte
- Project Manager: Dan Phillips
- Research Partners: London Borough of Greenwich; Innovate UK; Centre for Connected and Autonomous Vehicles; TRL

Connected Car

Helen Hamlyn Research Associates Programme 2009

- Research Associate: Filip Krnja
- Research Leads: Rama Gheerawo, Onny Eikhaug
- Research Partners: TH!NK; Norwegian Design Council; Research Council of Norway

Urban Moving 2030

Helen Hamlyn Research Associates Programme

- Shaun Hutchinson (2001) with Ford

Mobilicity

Helen Hamlyn Research Associates Programme

- Merih Kunur (2004) with Capoco Design

Save Your Sight

Helen Hamlyn Research Associates Programme

- Gero Grundman (2004) with Guide Dogs

Info-Motion

Helen Hamlyn Research Associates Programme

- Serge Porcher (2005) with Visteon

Keep Driving Safely

Helen Hamlyn Research Associates Programme

- John-Paul Baptiste (2007) with Toyota and Help the Aged

Wheelchair

Morph Wheel

Helen Hamlyn Student Design Award Winner 2007

- Designer: Duncan Fitzsimons
- Industry Partners: InnovationRCA; Maddak Inc.

The Abilizer

Helen Hamlyn Research Associates Programme 2000

- Research Associate: Judith Anderson
- Research Partner: Laura Ashley Foundation

Tilting Trike

Helen Hamlyn Research Associates Programme 2002

- Research Associate: Ben Wilson
- Research Partner: Whizz-Kidz

Acknowledgements

As this book covers a 30-year period, there are a lot of people I want to thank. Lady Hamlyn, Lucy O'Rorke and the Helen Hamlyn Trust have been wonderfully supportive in making this publication happen just as they have been wonderfully supportive throughout the many years of collaboration with the Royal College of Art. Roger Coleman and Rama Gheerawo, the only people apart from me to know what it's like to lead the Helen Hamlyn Centre for Design, have given invaluable advice.

The Centre's archive, on which this book draws heavily, was expertly created by Margaret Durkan, who together with Kay Sandford-Beale and Mark Byrne provided great operational support during my time as Director. Many of the concepts in the book owe their genesis to the members of our research team, past and present, who have always pushed the boundaries of inclusive design. I want to thank Julia Cassim, Jo-Anne Bichard, Ed Matthews, Yanki Lee, Gail Ramster, Chris McGinley, Jonathan West, Ninela Ivanova, John Bound, Alison Wright, Cherie Lebbon and Katie Gaudion (my first successful PhD candidate) for their ability to think in a new way.

Four Rectors of the Royal College of Art, Jocelyn Stevens, Tony Jones, Christopher Frayling and Paul Thompson, played an important role in shaping the creative environment in which the Helen Hamlyn Centre for Design could flourish. I have had the pleasure of working with so many talented RCA graduates on the Helen Hamlyn Research Associates Programme over the years – far too many to mention by name – but I've tried to capture at least some of your outstanding work in the pages of this book. I want to thank all RCA professors and faculty members who have participated in our programmes and our many academic, industry and advisory partners who are listed in this book. Among them is Colum Lowe who instigated some of our most important work in healthcare and today leads our Design Age Institute.

I also want to acknowledge the sterling work done by Ivelina Gadzheva on picture research and the professional efforts of the publications team at Lund Humphries led by Val Rose. Finally, my gratitude to my family, Wendy, Matthew and Nathan, who have been with me along every step of the journey over the past 30 years.

Jeremy Myerson,
London, 2021

Index

Note: **bold** page numbers indicate illustrations.

Abilizer wheelchair 129–31, **129**, 140
acoustic arch (Heathrow Airport) 5, 6, 12–13, **13**, 15
'Ageing in a Vertical City' study 38, **40**, 133
ambulances 4, 9, 16–21, **17**, **18–19**, **20**, **21**, 132
Anderson, Judith 129–131, **129**, 140
arthritis 50, **50**, 68–69, **68**, **69**
Atkin, Ross **106**, **112**, 138, 139
Audi Design Foundation 44, 119, 133, 139
Aura Power Suit 54, **56**, **57**, 135
autism 10, 51–52, 134
autonomous vehicles 9, 120–122, **120**, **121**, **122**, **124–125**, **127**, 139–140

B&Q 9, 89, **89**, 90, 138
Balance (stairlift project/app) 107–108, **108**, 138–139
banks, hybrid 22–25, **23**, **24**, **25**, 132
bathrooms 4, 7, 8, 26–31, **28**, **29**, 132
beer glasses 7, 32–33, **32**, **33**, 132–133
Bichard, Jo-Anne 91, 137, 138, 141
Blackberry 79, **80**, 137
British Airports Authority (BAA) 12, 13, 15
BT 77, **79**, 137
bus stops 34–35, **34**, **35**, 133

care homes 7, 36–41, **36**, **37**, **38**, **39**, **40–41**, 133
Carecentre unit 58, 60, **60–61**, 135
Cassim, Julia 9, 133, 135, 137, 138, 139, 141

Chalk (mobile phone project) 79, **80**, 137
children **70**, **130**, 131, **131**, 134, 140
classrooms 42–43, **42**, **43**, 133
Coleman, Roger 7, 8, 9, 135, 141
Connected Car project 121, 139
crutches 7, 44–45, **44**, **45**, 133

dementia 37, 102, 133
DePuy Johnson & Johnson 62, **65**, 136
Design Bridge 32, 33, 133
Design Bugs Out project 62, **64**, 135
Design Business Association (DBA) 8, 9, 133, 136, 138, 139
   Inclusive Design Challenge 9, 35, 69, 77, 88, 111, 134, 135, 137
Design Council 33, 60, 111, 133, 135
Design Museum 7, 17, **56**, 102, 134, 135, 138
Design for Patient Dignity project **64**, **67**, 135
DesignAge programme 4, 8, 9
desks 46–48, **47**, **48**, 134
disabled people 7, 49, 54, **55**, 77, **77**, **87**, 109
   see also Scooter for Life; stairlifts; streetscapes; wheelchairs
drugs packaging 74–76, **74**, **76**
dyslexia 7, **118**, 119

electric cars 7, 121–122, **123**, 139–140
'Ello (mobile phone project) 77, **77**, 137
ethnographic research 8, 26, 46, 49–50, 89, **90**

Factory Design 50, 69, **69**, 134, 136
Fitzsimmons, Duncan **128**, 129, 140
food packaging 49–50, **49**, **50**, 134
Ford 122, **123**, 140
Foyle, River see Our Future Foyle project
Frensch, Natasha **118**, 119, 139
furniture 8, **15**, 43, **43**
   see also desks
Fusari, Gianpaolo **20**, 132, 135
Fuseproject 54, **56**, 135

gardens 51–52, **51**, **52**, 134
garments, smart 9, 53–57, **53**, **54**, **55**, **56**, **57**, 135
GATEway project **120**, **121**, 139
Gaudion, Katie 10, 52, 134, 141
Gheerawo, Rama 9, 133, 137, 138, 139, 141
GlaxoSmithKline 75, **76**, 137, 138
Go Steady campaign 109–111, **109**, 139
Gofer (screwdriver) 89–90, **89**
Grcic, Konstantin 46–48, **48**, 134
Greene, Catherine **10–11**, **83**, 137

Hamlyn, Helen 4, 5, 8, 9, 141
Hansgrohe 26, **31**, 132
Head in the Sky workspace 48, **48**, 134
Heathrow Airport 5, 6, 12–15, **13**, **14**, **15**, 132
Helen Hamlyn Research Associates 8, 9, **10–11**, 141
Helen Hamlyn Trust 9, 21, 132, 141
Henderson, Elisabeth 4, 8

INDEX

Hexagon 114, 115, 139
hospitals 7, 9, 58–67, **59**, **60–61**, **62**, **63**, **64**, **65**, **66**, **67**, **74**, **76**, 135
see also ambulances
Hutchinson, Shaun 122, **123**, 140

Ideal Standard 26, **27**, **28**, 132
Imagination 87–88, **87**, **88**, 138
Impact Wave biker jacket 53–54, **53**, **54**
Imperial College London 9, 58, 135
Inspiration Park (London) 87–88, **87**, **88**, 138

Jar We Can Open 7, 49, **49**, 134
Jarvis, Tom 71–73, **84**, 136, 138

Karsan 114, 115, 139
Kecman, Maja **11**, **80**, 135, 136, 137
Kingwood College/Trust **51**, 52, **52**, 134
kitchens 4, 8, 68–69, **68**, **69**, 136
konro (Japanese stoves) 69, **69**, 136
Kunur, Merih 122, **122**, 139, 140

Lacock Gullam 34, **34**, 35, 133
Leonard Cheshire 46, **48**, 134
Levi Strauss 53–54, **53**, 135
lighting 7, 35, 37, **42**, **43**, 70–73, **70**, **71**, **72**, **73**, 133, 136

McGinley, Chris **69**, 133, 134, 136, 137, 139, 141
Marks & Spencer 49–50, 134
Mathias, Julie **28**, **29**, 132
medication *see* drugs packaging
milk cartons 50, **50**, 134
mobile phones 77–80, **77**, **78**, **79**, 137
Mobilicity project 122, **122**, 140
mobility scooters *see* Scooter for Life
Morph wheel **128**, 129, 140
Muhammad, Yusuf **80**, 132, 135, 137
Myerson, Jeremy **57**, 132, 133, 134, 135, 137, 138

National Patient Safety Agency (NPSA) 16, 74, **74**, 135, 136, 137
neck braces **11**, 62, **62**, 136

New Design for Old exhibition (Boilerhouse Gallery) 4, 7, 8, 9
New Old exhibition (Design Museum) **57**, 102, 135, 138
NHS (National Health Service) 9, 16, 44, 45, 74–75, 132, 135, 136
Nokia 79, **80**, 137

offices 71, 81–86, **81**, **83**, **84–85**, **86**, 137–138
older people 6, 22, 49–50, 54, **56**, 75, 91, 109, **126**
and kitchens/bathrooms 8, 26–31, **31**, 68–69, **68**, **69**
and mobile phones 77–79, **77**, **78**, **79**
and power tools 89–90, **89**, **90**
see also care homes
Our Future Foyle project 7, 94–101, **94**, **95**, **96–97**, **98–99**, **100–101**, 138

parks 87–8, **87**, **88**, 138
patient safety 58, 60, 64, **65**, 74–75, **74**, **76**
Pearlfisher 54, **55**, 135
playgrounds **70**, 71, 73, 134
power tools 8, 89–90, **89**, **90**, 138
Priestman, Paul/Priestman Goode 102, **103**, **104–105**, 138
Privett, Imogen **84–85**, 132, 138
public toilets 6, 7, 13, 91–93, **92**, **93**, 138

Quantified Self as the Qualified Self (QLS) 79, 137

Ramster, Gail 91, **93**, 138, 139, 141
Read type family **118**, 119, **119**, 139
Resus:station 58–60, **59**, 135
riverfronts *see* Our Future Foyle project
Robinson, Guy 44, **44**, 133
Rockware Glass 49, **49**, 134
Royal College of Art (RCA) 4, 5, 7, 8, 101, 119, 129, 132, 140, 141
Rygalik, Tomek **27**, **28**, 132

Samsung 77, **78**, 137
Sandbug (sander) 89, **89**, **90**

saucepans 69, **69**
Scooter for Life 102–105, **102**, **103**, **104–105**, 138
Scott, Fiona **110**, 139
Senso (digital app) 60, **63**, 135
Seymour Powell 77, **77**, 137
Sight Line project **112**, 139
Spencer, Jak 97, 138
Stables, Tom **11**
stairlifts 106–108, **106**, **107**, **108**, 138–139
Stannah Stairlifts 107, 108, 138, 139
streetscapes 4, 7, 109–113, **110**, **112**, **113**, 139
surgical tools 64, **65**, 136
SWIG (Safe Ways With Glass) project 33

taxis 114–117, **114**, **115**, **116**, **117**, 139
TH!NK project 121, **123**, 139
tilting trike **130**, 131, **131**, 140
Timlin, Gregor **36**, **37**, 133
Togetherness project 38, 133
Torlei, Karina **11**, 135, 136
Two-Tone Phone 77, **79**, 137
typefaces 118–119, **118**, **119**, 139

UniCredit 22, 23, **23**, 132

Vaananen, Lotta **48**, 134
Visteon 122, **125**, 140
visually impaired people 22, 34, 35, 79, **80**, 89, 111, **112**, **113**, 140

Wagstaff, Mary **31**, 132
Watergate bath **30**, **31**, 132
Welcoming Workplace study 81–82, **81**
West, Jonathan **58**, 135, 138, 141
Westaway, Clara Gaggero/ Westaway, Adrian **78**, 137
wheelchairs 8, 44, 46, **48**, 87, 88, 109, 128–131, **128**, **130**, **131**, 140
White, Matthew **89**, 90, 138
Whizz-Kidz 131, 140
Wilson, Ben **130**, 131, 140
Wolff Olins 109–110, **109**, 139
Work at Home project 46, 134
Workscapes project **86**, 138

Illustration Credits

Foreword: Images courtesy of Helen Hamlyn Centre for Design and Royal College of Art (pp 4–5).
Introduction: All images by Petr Krejčí (pp 10–11).
Airport: Drawings by Carl Turner and Karen Adcock (p13, p16); installation by Samson Adjei and Pascal Anson (p14); Heathrow Terminal 5 image by Nick Fewings, Unsplash (p14). **Ambulance:** Image courtesy of NHS England (p17); images by Petr Krejčí (pp 18–19, p20); images by Gianpaolo Fusari (p21). **Bank:** All layouts and visualisations by Andrew Thompson (pp 23–25); image courtesy of Klaus Sandbiller, UniCredit (p23). **Bathroom:** Images courtesy of Ideal Standard (p27, p28); visuals by Julie Mathias (p28, p29), Barnaby Barford (p30, p31) and Mary Wagstaff (p31). **Beer Glass:** All images courtesy of Design Bridge (pp 32–33). **Bus Stop:** Images by Lacock Gullam (pp 34–35). **Care Home:** Image by Petr Krejčí (p36); images courtesy of Gregor Timlin (p37), Nick Rysenbry (p38), Lisa Johansson (p39) and Rama Gheerawo/Hong Kong Polytechnic University (pp 40–41). **Classroom:** Images by Amanda Buckley (p42) and Mark Champkins (p43). **Crutch:** All images by Guy Robinson (pp 44–45). **Desk:** Images courtesy of Peter Fullager and Dan Jones (p47), Lotta Vaanenen (p48) and Konstain Grcic (p48). **Food Pack:** Images courtesy of DesignAge (p49), Edward Goodwin and Richard Hartshorn (p50) and Factory Design/Julia Cassim (p50). **Garden:** Illustration by Sasha Mihajlovic (p51); photographs by Katie Gaudion (p52); graphic by Chris McGinley (p52). **Garment:** Images courtesy of Dan Plant (p53, p54), Pearlfisher/Julia Cassim (p55), Yves Behar/Fuseproject (pp 56–57) and Kaohsiung Museum of Fine Arts, Taiwan (p57). **Hospital:** Images by Petr Krejčí (p58, pp 60–61, p62) and Jonathan West/Bristol Maid (p59); images courtesy of Design Council (p62, p64); images by Gabriele Meldaikyte (p63), Maja Kecman/De Puy Johnson and Johnson (p65), Pearson Lloyd (p66); visuals courtesy of Design Council/Department of Health (p67). **Kitchen:** Images by Simon Kinneir (p68), Factory Design (page 69) and Chris McGinley (p69). **Light:** Images by Tom Jarvis (p70, p71); illustration by Matthew Dearlove (p72); image courtesy of Harry Dobbs Design (p73). **Medication:** Image courtesy of NPSA England (p74); image courtesy of Thea Swayne (p75); image by Richard Mawle/Chris McGinley. **Mobile Phone:** Images courtesy of Seymour Powell (p77), Clara Gaggero Westaway/Adrian Westaway/Special Projects (p78), Matthew Harrison (p79), Julia Cassim (p80) and Yusuf Muhammad p80). **Office:** Images by Catherine Greene (p81, p83); image courtesy of Haworth London (p84); visuals by Imogen Privett (p85), Benjamin Koslowski and Lottie Crumbleholme (p86). **Park:** All visuals courtesy of Imagination/Julia Cassim (pp 87–88). **Power Tool:** Images courtesy of B&Q (p89) and Matthew White (p90). **Public Toilet:** Images courtesy of Gail Ramster/Public Convenience (p91, p92); photo by Petr Krejčí (p93). **River:** Images by Ralf Alwani, Greg Edwards, Urban Scale Interventions (pp 94–101). **Scooter:** All images courtesy of Priestman Goode (pp 102–105). **Stairlift:** Images by Petr Krejčí (p106), Ross Atkins and Shruti Grover (pp 107–108). **Street:** Images courtesy of Wolff Olins (p109), Fiona Scott (p110), Ellie Risdale (p111) and Ross Atkins (pp 112–113). **Taxi:** Images by Peter Stevens and Intelligent Mobility Design (pp 114–115); images courtesy of Dale Harrow, Karsan and Hexagon (pp 116–117). **Typeface:** Images courtesy of Natasha Frensch (pp 118–119). **Vehicle:** Images created by Paul Piliste, copyright RCA (pp 120–121); illustrations by Merih Kunur (p122), Shaun Hutchinson and Filip Krnja (p123); image by Dan Phillips (p124); photo courtesy of Serge Porcher (p125); illustration by Gero Grundman (p126); icons by Daniel Quinlan, Samuel Johnson (p127); posters by Jean Paul Baptiste, with Jim Sutherland (p127). **Wheelchair:** Images courtesy of Duncan Fitzsimons (p128), Judith Anderson (p129) and Ben Wilson/The Light Surgeons (pp 130–131).